a smart girl's guide

Cooking

how to make food for your friends, your family & yourself

by Patricia Daniels and Darcie Johnston
illustrated by Elisa Chavarri

Published by American Girl Publishing
All rights reserved. No part of this book may be used or reproduced
in any manner whatsoever without written permission except in the
case of brief quotations embodied in critical articles and reviews.

16 17 18 19 20 21 22 23 LEO 10 9 8 7 6 5 4 3 2 1

Editorial Development: Darcie Johnston
Art Direction and Design: Gretchen Becker
Illustrations: Elisa Chavarri
Production: Jeannette Bailey, Laura Markowitz, Cynthia Stiles, Kristi Tabrizi
Consultant: Kevin Appleton

Library of Congress Cataloging-in-Publication Data
Daniels, Patricia, 1955-
Cooking : how to make food for your friends, your family & yourself /
by Patricia Daniels and Darcie Johnston ; illustrated by Elisa Chavarri.
    pages   cm — (A smart girl's guide)
ISBN 978-1-60958-736-9 (pbk. : alk. paper) — ISBN 978-1-60958-759-8 (ebook)
1. Cooking—Juvenile literature.
I. Johnston, Darcie. II. Chavarri, Elisa, illustrator. III. Title.
TX652.5.D355 2016   641.5—dc23   2015022682

Safety Note
Even though instructions have been tested and results from testing were incor-
porated into this book, all recommendations and suggestions are made without
any guarantees on the part of American Girl. Because of differing tools, materials,
ingredients, conditions, and individual skills, the publisher disclaims liability for
any injuries, losses, or other damages that may result from using the information
in this book. Knives, ovens and stoves, hot dishes and ingredients, uncooked food,
and powered appliances can cause severe injury. **Adult supervision is required
at all times when following any instruction in this book.**

americangirl.com/service

Dear Reader,

Maybe you already love bustling in the kitchen. Maybe you want to, but you think it's hard or scary. Maybe you never give a thought to how food is made when you open your lunch or ask what's for dinner. Whichever girl you are, this book is for you. It's about more than what recipe to cook. This book will show you *how* to cook.

Why do you want to know how? Let's count the ways.
1. Cooking is creative and fun.
2. It's easy. Anyone can learn—including you.
3. Sharing a snack or a meal with family or friends is one of the joys of life.
4. Knowing how to cook means you get to choose what you eat. Yum!
5. Making your own food keeps you healthier, because you decide what to put in your body.
6. When you're older, you'll care that it saves you time and money.
7. Cooking is cool!

In this book, you'll learn the basics that will set you on the road to cooking independence: what those pots and pans are for, how to handle tools like a pro, how to measure flour and peel a carrot and roast a chicken. Also: how to read a recipe top to bottom, how to shop smart, and how to plan a meal from savory start to sweet finish. You may even pick up some clever cooking tips that your parents don't know. And you'll learn to do it all safely, because staying safe is the first and last rule of cooking.

So let's get cracking!

Your friends at American Girl

contents

food, glorious food......6

join the club

family traditions

the joys of cooking

QUIZ your cooking sense

happy & healthy

the staples

different foods for different folks

tools & rules...26

the safe kitchen

TOOLS

pots & pans

knives, peelers & graters

bowls & other basics

best for baking

small appliances & gadgets

how-to basics.........42

measuring ingredients

handling knives

slicing & dicing

peeling, grating & zesting

keeping it clean

mixing it up

breaking it up

rolling it out

get cracking!..64

ready, set, cook!

hot terms

how to read a recipe

RECIPES
    easy eggs
    fruit smoothies
    great basics
    beautiful bird
    fish feast
    gorgeous greens
    veggies two ways
    sweet treats

cooking 911: help for kitchen emergencies

it happened to me!

from soup to nuts......94

thinking ahead

mind over menus

recipe finds

MENUS
    the lunchbox
    family dinners
    birthday bashes
    breakfast bites

making a list, checking it twice

let's go shopping!

table time

SAFETY NOTE

Almost every technique and recipe in this book involves heat, sharp tools such as knives, powered appliances, or raw food (which may have germs). Adult supervision is required at all times and for all instructions and recipes.

join the club

What's your favorite meal?

Zippy hot tacos on a Saturday night?

The spaghetti and meatballs your mom makes for your birthday?

Turkey, stuffing, and all the trimmings at Thanksgiving?

These are more than meals. They are also memories. Cooking means sharing in traditions that go back thousands of years.

Family recipes hold family history. Maybe your great-grandmother brought that pasta recipe with her from Rome. Maybe your dad learned to make his tacos in Texas when he was a kid. Wherever they came from, those recipes contain stories about your own past.

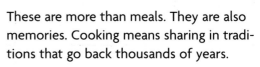

Cooking passes on world history, too. Every culture expresses itself with its own special foods. When you're eating hummus, spring rolls, or curry, you're experiencing other places in the tastiest way.

You can join that great tradition. It's easy. Not only can you learn to make family favorites, but you can invent your own mouthwatering dishes, too.

The more you cook, the more you'll get to know how foods and flavors go together, and how to change things up the way you like. One day you won't even need a recipe—except when you want to try something really different.

Cooking is old, yet at the same time, for a creative cook, cooking is always new.

Welcome to the club!

family traditions

Do you and your family eat a special holiday meal, handed down for generations? Or do you have fun food traditions that you invented yourselves? Here's what girls have to share about their own family traditions.

Every year, my family and I—including my mom, sister, cousin, grandma, and aunts—make hundreds of homemade ravioli to eat at holidays and birthday dinners. They are the most delicious ravioli ever tasted, hands down!

—Rosita

For Hanukkah, my mom always makes her own donuts and potato pancakes.

—Rachel

At Christmas, my mama makes tamales and posole. Posole is a Mexican soup that has hominy, meat, and a spicy broth. Tamales have masa on the outside and spicy sauce and meat on the inside. They're delicious!

—Naya

I'm from Sweden, and we always make saffron buns for the holiday Saint Lucia. The buns are shaped like an **S** and have raisins. Saint Lucia brings light to the darkest time of the year!

—Caroline

We have spaghetti for dinner every Monday night. It always gives me something to look forward to on the first day of the school week!

—Katie

My family makes monkey bread for any special holiday. My mom makes it, my mom's mom makes it, and my mom's mom's mom makes it, too!

—Tyler

My grandma has a recipe called Czech puzzle cookies. They are crunchy and have powdered sugar all over them, and they're so good! Best of all, she passed the recipe down to my sister and me.

—Erin

For our tradition, my family always has a Sunday night dinner. I like it because this is a time every week when I get to be with my sister and brother, who are gone a lot. We always have a special home-cooked meal.

—Madelyn

About once a month, my mom or dad will serve one of us kids on a special bright red plate. When someone gets the special plate, each family member will say one good thing about him or her while we eat dinner.

—Eva

My family celebrates Eid. Girls wear clothes called *salwar kameez*, and everyone eats a rice dish called *biryani* and a dessert called *mitai*.

—Sania

the joys of cooking

What's so great about cooking? Let's see . . .

Cooking is fun!

It gives you a zillion chances to explore and experiment. Comb through cookbooks and websites for dishes that get you excited. Discover the foods of other countries and cultures. Be creative with flavors and food combinations. There's no end to the pleasures you'll find.

Cooking brings people together.

Sure, you can make something just for yourself. But cooking is a great way to have fun with friends and family. Put on some music and pull your pals into the kitchen. Decorate cupcakes. Create personal pizzas. Mash up guacamole. Take your place among the family's holiday cooks and show what you can do.

Cooking keeps you healthy and strong.

When you make your own meals, you're eating fresh food that you know is good, not mystery ingredients from plastic packages. If you're the cook, you're more likely to know what's really on your plate—and to care.

Cooking puts you in charge.

When you know how to make your own meals, you're the boss. You can design your own lunches. You can cook just what you like for friends. You don't have to rely on someone else. You're the chef!

Cooking is delicious.

Making—and eating—scrumptious homemade food is one of life's great pleasures. It just is.

your cooking sense

Which of these scenes describes you the best?

1. The French bread recipe calls for 1 tablespoon of sugar. You . . .

a. use a cereal spoon to add a heap of sugar to the mixing bowl.

b. add just enough sugar to fill up the cereal spoon, then dump the sugar into the bowl.

c. find the measuring spoon marked "1 T," fill it just to the rim, and add the sugar to the bowl.

2. You're supposed to "whisk" three eggs together. You . . .

a. crack the eggs into a bowl and use a cooking tool with wire loops to stir them until they're frothy.

b. crack the eggs into a bowl and blend them briskly (rhymes with *whiskly*) with a wooden spoon.

c. put three eggs in a bowl and hope for the best.

3. You're in charge of planning tonight's dinner. Your menu is . . .

a. rice, French fries, pizza, and mashed potatoes, because everybody loves those, right?

b. roast chicken, rice pilaf, and a big green salad.

c. something easy—maybe chicken nuggets and brownies?

4. It's time to start making your dad's favorite vegetable soup. The first thing you do is . . .

a. read the first step in the recipe and do what it says: Add carrots to the pot.

b. read the whole recipe, including the ingredients list, and realize that you have to peel and chop the carrots first. You do that and add them to the pot.

c. read the whole recipe, including the ingredients list. Then you measure, peel, and chop everything and have all the ingredients ready before you start cooking.

5. The cake batter is in the pans and ready to bake. You . . .

a. slide the pans into the heated oven and leave the kitchen. You'll remember to take them out. Probably.

b. slide the pans into the heated oven, set the timer, take out the pans to cool when they're done, and turn off the oven.

c. slide the pans into the heated oven, set the timer, and turn off the oven when they're done, leaving the pans in there. They'll stay nice and warm.

6. It's time for your morning smoothie. You . . .

a. make the same banana smoothie as always. Why mess with success?

b. read through a cookbook and decide you'll take a chance on a blueberry smoothie soon.

c. invent something new—new fruits, new yogurts, new combinations—every week!

Answers

1. If you chose **c**, you already know the difference between spoons used for measuring and spoons used for eating or stirring. Measuring spoons (and measuring cups) allow you to add exactly the right amount of an ingredient to a recipe. When you're baking something like bread or cake or cookies, it's especially important that measurements are precise. That's because the ingredients that make baked things deliciously puffy or chewy have to be in just the right amount to do their job. It's chemistry in action!

2. If you chose **a**, you know there are special tools and techniques for mixing ingredients together. A whisk is an actual gadget that's used to whip ingredients by hand when a spoon won't do. With a whisk, you can add air to eggs so they're light and fluffy, or mix oil and vinegar together into a creamy salad dressing, or make thick whipped cream from the liquid in the carton.

3. If you chose **b**, you have a good sense of what makes a meal both exciting and healthy. When planning a meal, cooks decide which foods from different food groups they'll include. (That's the healthy part.) They also think about ways to make a meal look yummy on the plate, such as combining colors and serving a pleasing variety of foods.

4. If you chose **c,** you realize that the best way to follow a recipe is to read it all the way through *before* you start cooking. Then you won't have any surprises. *("What? I was supposed to turn the oven on??")* Also, it gives you a chance to prepare your ingredients and have them ready so that you can time things right during the cooking part.

5. If you chose **b,** you probably have some experience with a regular oven. You know that when you turn the oven off, it stays hot for a while, so any food still in there will keep cooking. (A microwave oven, on the other hand, stops cooking the instant it turns off.)

6. If you chose **a, b,** or **c,** it's all good! Whether you love sticking with familiar favorites or trying new creations every day, making food is all about expressing yourself and discovering what you like.

happy & healthy

Apples are tasty and good for you. But if you ate only apples every day—apples for breakfast, apples for lunch, apples for dinner—you would turn into one. Well, maybe not. But you would be really, really sick and tired of apples.

There's a saying that goes, "Variety is the spice of life." It's true. Food is more fun if you're not eating the same thing all the time. Imagine your basic peanut butter sandwich—a little boring? But add some sweet banana or crispy apple slices, and it gets a lot more interesting. Now add maple cream cheese or raspberry jam, with or without the fruit. Or take away the bread and try it on graham crackers. Changing things up and adding ingredients with different colors, flavors, and textures makes food more appetizing. You can hardly wait to take a bite!

And that's not all. Variety doesn't just make you happy. It also makes you healthy. Different foods have different vitamins, minerals, and other nutrients that people need. Some build bones and muscles. Some boost your energy. Some help you see better, or fight off the flu, or give your skin a beautiful glow. And you need them all.

So when smart chefs decide what to cook, they think about what's both happy and healthy. They think variety. One easy way to do that is to choose foods from each of the main food groups— fruits, veggies, protein, grains, and dairy.

FRUITS

Scientifically speaking, a fruit is the part of a plant where seeds grow. *Foodishly* speaking, fruits are sweet, tart, or spicy—and some of the most delicious things ever! Pop fresh berries into your mouth. Bake cherries or apples or peaches into pies and crisps. Blend a banana or mango into a smoothie, or squeeze lemons into zesty lemonade. Fruits can add flavor and beauty (and vitamins) to just about anything.

VEGETABLES

Mmm-mmm-mashed potatoes. A cool green salad. Crisp carrots and corn on the cob and pumpkin pie. Like fruits, vegetables are also the part of a plant that you eat, such as its leaves or roots. Depending on how you make them, they're crunchy or creamy, sweet tasting or sharp. They're a great source of vitamins and minerals. And they come in every color of the rainbow, making a plate look deliciously fun.

PROTEIN

Foods from both plants and animals contain protein. Meat, fish, eggs, beans, nuts, and milk are the main sources. Think barbecued chicken, peanut butter, baked beans, grilled shrimp, a cheesy omelette, or a hamburger. It's good that protein is so easy to come by, because it's needed by your muscles, bones, skin, blood, hair, and even your fingernails—every cell in your body!

GRAINS

Warm-from-the-oven bread. Jasmine rice and pizza crust, noodles and tortillas. Sweet granola. Oatmeal cookies. Usually we eat grains cooked—baked into breads or cereals, boiled for pasta or soups, or steamed into pilafs. All grains come from plants, and they give you the energy to move, to think, and to run every system in the body.

Dairy

Cheeses, such as cheddar, feta, and mozzarella. Yogurt, ice cream, and pudding. A frosty shake or a mug of hot chocolate. Milk and foods made from milk are called the dairy group. They do double duty by counting in the protein group, too, but what makes dairy foods special is that they have lots of the mineral calcium. Without calcium, you wouldn't have bones or teeth!

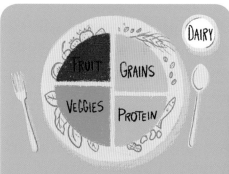

Plan with MyPlate

This cheerful plate shows you how much of which kind of food to eat each day. It also makes a great guide to planning meals for yourself, your family, and your friends. Fruits and vegetables take up half the plate, followed by grains, and then protein and dairy. You don't have to eat each meal like this, but keep the plate in mind over the course of a day or a week.

Girl Power

Two minerals are really important for girls: calcium and iron. Calcium builds strong bones, and iron helps your blood carry oxygen around your body. Dairy foods are the richest source of calcium, but broccoli, almonds, and many beans are good, too. For iron, great sources are eggs, red meat, and broccoli. (Broccoli—a calcium and iron twofer!)

the staples

The fridge and pantry are filled with foods that are always there, waiting to be added to anything from artichoke dip to zucchini bread. When you need a splash of olive oil or a teaspoon of cinnamon, you just reach for them. When you run out, you get more right away. Ingredients like these are called *staples*.

Fats

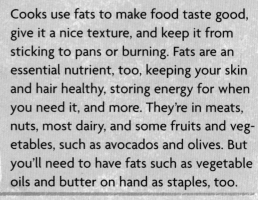

Cooks use fats to make food taste good, give it a nice texture, and keep it from sticking to pans or burning. Fats are an essential nutrient, too, keeping your skin and hair healthy, storing energy for when you need it, and more. They're in meats, nuts, most dairy, and some fruits and vegetables, such as avocados and olives. But you'll need to have fats such as vegetable oils and butter on hand as staples, too.

Salt Box

Salt sharpens flavor—even though it isn't food. It's a chemical compound called sodium chloride, which is found in the ground as rock salt or dissolved in seawater. Every animal and plant contains some salt, too—ever notice how salty your tears or sweat is? Without salt, muscles and nerves wouldn't work right. Just don't overdo it in food, because too much is bad for you. The tongue is designed to taste small amounts of salt, so go light on it when you cook. It's easy to add salt to food, but really hard to take it out.

Seasonings

Savory and sweet: These are the two basic kinds of seasonings. Salt and pepper are used in nearly every savory dish, and sugar or honey is added to most sweet foods. To enhance and fine-tune flavors, most recipes also call for certain spices, herbs, and plant extracts that you'll want to keep on hand.

Oregano · CHILI POWDER · Rosemary · THYME · Curry · Parsley · PAPRIKA · CUMIN · Cinnamon · Pure Vanilla

EXTRA Virgin OLIVE OIL · CANOLA Oil · COOKING SPRAY · olive oil · CORN STARCH · SALT FROM the SEA · BAKING SODA · BAKING POWDER · pure cane Sugar · All Purpose FLOUR · HONEY

Fresh or Dried?

Fresh herbs and spices are delicious. They don't last long, though, so having dried versions in the cupboard means you've got what you need in a pinch. If a recipe calls for fresh or dried, and you plan to use the other, you'll need to adjust the amount, because dried versions are usually more intense than fresh.

Using dried instead of fresh?
Add about ⅓ what the recipe says.

Using fresh instead of dried?
Add about 3 times more.

different foods for different folks

You're at the cafeteria with friends, and nobody orders the same thing. You choose the hamburger with lettuce, tomato, and pickles. Your BFF never eats meat; she asks for the grilled cheese and black beans. Another girl has fruit salad and a turkey sandwich but says hold the cheese—she's allergic to dairy.

You make choices every time you cook or eat, and some of those choices involve particular kinds of *diets*.

Omnivores eat both plant and animal foods. ("Omni" is Latin for "all," and "vore" comes from a Latin word meaning "to eat.")

Vegetarians usually don't eat any kind of meat or fish, but they do eat other protein-rich foods that come from animals, such as milk, cheese, and eggs.

Vegans follow a stricter diet than vegetarians. They don't eat meat, fish, or any animal products, including dairy, eggs, or honey. Vegans get their protein from plant sources such as beans, nuts, and tofu.

Flexitarians have a mostly vegetarian diet, but they occasionally eat fish or meat such as chicken.

Sometimes people follow special diets for health reasons. People who have trouble digesting grains such as wheat or barley will eat a gluten-free diet. (Gluten is a protein found in some grains.) They avoid breads, cookies, or pastas made with regular flour but can eat these foods if they're made with gluten-free flours such as rice flour or cornmeal.

Lots of people have food allergies, too. Eating even a tiny bit of a particular food—such as peanuts, shellfish, milk, or eggs—can be dangerous to them.

People also follow special diets for religious reasons. For instance, Jewish and Islamic traditions forbid eating pork, and many Hindus will not eat beef or are completely vegetarian.

The good cook's rule of thumb: Always check with your guests about allergies and traditions before planning a meal.

25

tools
& rules

the safe kitchen

Kitchen tools make it all happen. They can chop and slice food, measure it and mix it together, and blast it with heat, transforming it into dishes you drool over. But if you don't know how to use them, or if you're not careful with them, some can hurt you. So read the rules before you touch the tools.

Rule #1 Cook with an adult. Always. And learn how to handle sharp stuff, hot stuff, and raw stuff before you get started.

Begin by taking a kitchen tour with an adult. Learn what your appliances do. Practice turning them on and off. Ask about the different settings. What's "purée" on the blender? What's "power level" on the microwave? What does "broil" mean on the oven? And find out how to use a kitchen timer so the buzzer can remind you when something is ready.

- Loose hair
- Dangling sleeves
- Loose clothes
- Earrings
- Scarf
- Necklace
- Bracelets
- Rings
- Flip-flops

Tip
Your kitchen counters may be too high for comfortable cooking. A sturdy stepstool can bring you up to the right level.

Rule #2 Dress up—up and away from stove tops and counters, that is. Dangling hair, clothes, and jewelry can catch fire or get caught in appliances. Keep everything rolled up, tied back, and tucked away. If you wear an apron, make sure it's snug and fastened behind your back. And wear closed shoes. Bare toes are targets for hot sauces and heavy pans.

- Hair tied back
- Sleeves rolled up
- No earrings
- Nothing around neck
- Bare wrists and hands
- Closed-toe shoes
- Close-fitting apron tied in back

29

Rule #3 Stay focused on the task at hand. If your attention wanders, you might end up saying, "What's that burning smell?" Or worse, "OUCH!"

Tip

An apron isn't necessary for safety, but it does help you stay clean. If you wear one, you can focus on food—instead of the stain you just got on your favorite shirt!

Rule #4 Keep clean. The first thing to do every time you cook is wash your hands with soap. The last thing is wash the dishes—and your hands again. In between, be careful to keep raw meat and eggs away from other foods so that germs don't spread. Always wash your hands after touching them—and countertops and any tools, too. (More about that on pages 54–57.)

Rule #5 Be cool. Hot stove tops, ovens, and microwaves can burn you, even if they don't look hot. Handle hot stuff only with an adult's permission and only with that adult standing right there with you.

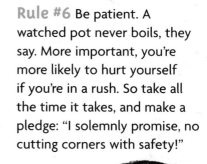

Rule #6 Be patient. A watched pot never boils, they say. More important, you're more likely to hurt yourself if you're in a rush. So take all the time it takes, and make a pledge: "I solemnly promise, no cutting corners with safety!"

Rule #7 Stay sharp. Don't pick up a knife unless you have an adult with you AND you know how to handle it safely. (More about that on pages 46–50.)

pots & pans

Pots and pans come in all shapes and sizes. Like Goldilocks, you want to pick the right one—not too big, not too small, but *juuust* right.

Also called a frying pan, a skillet is a shallow pan used to cook foods on the stove top. Some have nonstick coatings. Some have sloped sides, and some have straight sides. The kind with straight sides is best for cooking sauces and other things that slosh around.

Non-Sense

If you're cooking with high heat on the stove, do not use nonstick cookware. At very hot temperatures, nonstick coatings give off chemicals that are bad for you. But cooking with nonstick pans on low or medium heat is fine. Always use wood or plastic tools that won't scratch the coating.

Sometimes a recipe says you should use a nonreactive pot or pan. Stainless steel, enameled iron, and glass pans are nonreactive, and so are most pans with a nonstick coating. Pots that are reactive include unlined copper, aluminum, and cast iron. When acid foods such as fruits are cooked in them, these metals dissolve a tiny bit into the food, which can be unhealthy to eat.

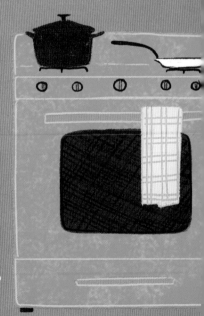

Saucepans can be big or small, deep or shallow. These multi-purpose pans with long handles are good for making sauces and soups and for boiling pasta, rice, and other foods. They usually come with matching covers.

When you're making lots of soup, broth, or pasta, you might reach for a large, tall, straight-sided stockpot.

Usually made of cast iron with an enamel coating, heavy Dutch ovens with lids are good for cooking meats or vegetables in liquid either on the stove top or in the oven.

A roasting pan is a wide metal pan for cooking large pieces of meat, such as a Thanksgiving turkey, in the oven. Some have lids.

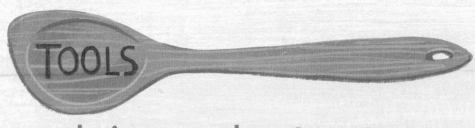

TOOLS

knives, peelers & graters

Knives are a cook's most basic tools. Chefs use them for everything from slicing meat to mincing garlic into tiny bits. Other sharp tools are used to remove tough rinds and skins and to shred hard foods. Follow the safety rules about tools that cut—and stay sharp!

A chef's knife slices and chops firm foods, such as vegetables. These knives, which come in different sizes, all have a smooth, rounded bottom edge.

A bread knife (also called a *serrated* knife) has a scalloped or wavy edge. You'll use a sawing motion with this knife to slice soft foods, such as bread or tomatoes, without crushing them.

The short, pointed paring knife is good for small, precise kinds of cutting, like slicing the stem from a mushroom.

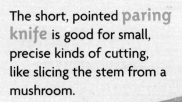

Vegetable peelers scrape the tough skin off vegetables such as carrots and potatoes. They come in two basic styles: slender vertical peelers and Y-shaped peelers that have a horizontal blade.

When you slide a firm food such as hard cheese down the side of a grater, the sharp edges cut the food into bits. Most graters have different-sized holes to give you larger or smaller pieces.

TOOLS

bowls & other basics

Whether you're grabbing, scooping, spinning, straining, or mixing, there's a handy tool for every task.

Mixing bowls come in different sizes and materials, including ceramic, plastic, and metal. You use them to mix ingredients or simply hold them before cooking.

A **salad spinner** rinses salad greens and then spins them dry. It's also handy for rinsing and draining other veggies and fruits.

A **colander** drains the liquids off of foods. For instance, you would drain a pot of cooked spaghetti in a colander.

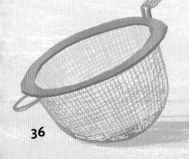

A **strainer** is usually smaller than a colander and has finer holes. Strainers hold small solid bits and let water and other thin liquids drain through.

The holes in a slotted spoon let liquid run through. These spoons are great for fishing pieces of food out of a cooking liquid.

With its deep bowl, a ladle is useful for spooning up soups and stews.

Cooking spoons are made from wood, plastic, or metal and are a basic tool for stirring foods on the stove top or mixing ingredients in a bowl.

A liquid measuring cup measures liquid ingredients such as water, milk, or oil. It's made of clear glass or plastic so you can see exactly how much liquid is inside. These cups are usually marked in fractions of a cup, in ounces, and in milliliters.

Dry measuring cups measure dry ingredients, such as flour or sugar. Usually these come in sets ranging in size from ¼ cup to 1 cup.

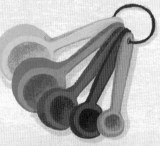

Measuring spoons measure small amounts of ingredients such as spices. Sets of spoons typically come in sizes from ⅛ teaspoon to 1 tablespoon.

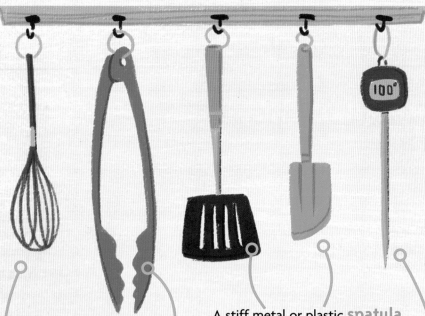

A stiff metal or plastic **spatula** (also called a *turner*) has a flat surface that lifts and flips pancakes, eggs, cookies, and other food from pans and baking sheets. A flexible rubber spatula is good for turning and mixing ingredients in a bowl. It may seem confusing that they have the same name, but you'll know which one to use.

Tongs let you pick up food by grasping it from the sides.

Usually made from loops of wire, a **whisk** is good at mixing ingredients together without forming lumps. It's also used to whip air into liquid ingredients, making them light and frothy or thick and creamy. Some whisks have a coating so you can use them without scratching non-stick or enamel surfaces.

When poked into meat or other food or liquids, an **instant-read thermometer** measures how hot something like roast chicken is on the inside.

Thermo-Matters

There are many different kinds of kitchen thermometers. Some are only for candy or for deep-frying. Know which kind you're using. Also, make sure you know which can be left in a hot oven and which ones will melt!

TOOLS

best for baking

For each of the many different foods that bake in the oven, there's a perfect pan for the job.

Loaf pans, made of metal, glass, or ceramic, come in various sizes and are used to bake foods like bread, meatloaf, and small cakes.

Cookies and pizza are just two of the many foods you can bake on flat metal **baking sheets** (also called *cookie sheets*).

Shallow, round **cake pans** are used to bake cake batter in the oven.

Made from glass or ceramics, **baking dishes** are useful for all kinds of oven-cooked foods, including meats, vegetables, and casseroles. Some have lids. Pretty ones double as serving dishes.

Just the thing for cupcakes or muffins, a **muffin pan** (also called a *muffin tin*) is a tray with cups for holding batter. Most have 6 or 12 cups.

Also called a *pie pan*, a **pie plate** is for baking— what else?—pies.

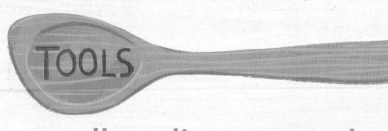

TOOLS

small appliances & gadgets

Small kitchen appliances can make your job a lot easier. Their sharp edges, moving parts, and hot elements can be dangerous, though, so always use them with an adult.

A **toaster** heats and browns two or more slices of bread or other bready food, such as bagels, using heating elements on the inside.

A **slow cooker** cooks soups, roasts, and other one-pot dishes at a low temperature over a period of several hours.

Food Processor?

A food processor has blades—some very, very sharp—that spin rapidly to chop, slice, and mix food. This machine isn't a kitchen necessity. Tools such as knives, graters, blenders, and mixers can do the same jobs just as well, with less danger. If there is one in your kitchen, never touch the removable blades, and always ask an adult to run it.

Give It a Spin

Know these guidelines for using mixers and blenders.

1. Make sure your hands are dry before you plug in or unplug an appliance.

2. Never stick your hand or a utensil into a spinning mixer or blender. Wait until it is completely stopped and unplugged. Make sure any utensil is removed if you need to turn it back on.

3. When you've added ingre-dients to a mixer, start it on the slowest speed. That way the contents won't fly out and splatter you—and the walls of your kitchen!

4. Always put the lid firmly on a blender before turning it on. (See the previous rule about splatter!)

A **stand mixer** uses different attachments to whip or mix large amounts of ingredients.

A **hand blender** is used to mix or blend right in the pot, bowl, or glass—without moving food to another container.

The sharp blades of a **blender** chop and mix ingredients in a narrow container.

The two spinning whisks of a **hand mixer** whip or mix small amounts of cream, eggs, batter, and other soft foods.

how-to basics

measuring ingredients

Almost every recipe asks you to measure ingredients. Maybe you'll need 1 cup of sugar for a cookie recipe or ¼ teaspoon of salt in your soup. Whenever you measure, remember these tips:

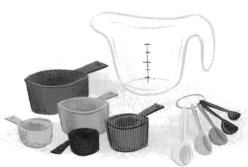

Tip #1 Use official measuring cups and spoons, not the tableware you eat with.

Tip #2 Use dry measuring cups for dry ingredients and wet measuring cups for wet ingredients. The same measuring spoons work for both wet and dry.

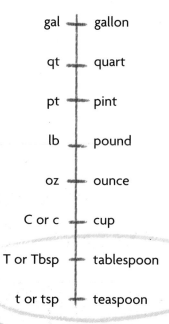

Abbreviations

Measuring tools and recipes often use abbreviations for measurements.

gal	gallon
qt	quart
pt	pint
lb	pound
oz	ounce
C or c	cup
T or Tbsp	tablespoon
t or tsp	teaspoon

Dry Ingredients

Spoon the ingredient (let's say, sugar) into the dry measuring cup until it overflows a bit. Don't pack it down unless the recipe says so. Then scrape the flat edge of a table knife across the top of the cup to sweep off the extra. If you're using a measuring spoon, dip it into the sugar, and then sweep off the extra in the same way.

Wet Ingredients

Put the clear liquid measuring cup on the counter, and pour in the liquid (let's say, milk). Then bend down and peer into the cup from the side, at eye level with the milk. Check that the liquid reaches the correct measuring line on the cup. Add more or pour some out, if necessary. (If you look at the milk from above, you won't get an accurate measurement. Try it and see!)

Special Cases

When measuring flour, first use your spoon to fluff it a little in the bag or bin before you measure. Then gently scoop the flour and place it in the measuring cup, nice and easy. Don't pack or press down on the flour.

Brown sugar is just the opposite. Scoop it into your measuring cup and press it down. Keep adding and pressing until the cup is full. Then press one more time to make sure it's as tightly packed as possible.

Just a Pinch

A *pinch* of an ingredient is roughly $1/16$ of a teaspoon—about as much as you can pick up between your thumb and forefinger. A *dash* is about $1/8$ of a teaspoon.

45

handling knives

Cooking and cutting go hand in hand—literally. If you're going to be in the kitchen fixing food, you'll be handling a knife. So let's meet one.

Chef's Knife

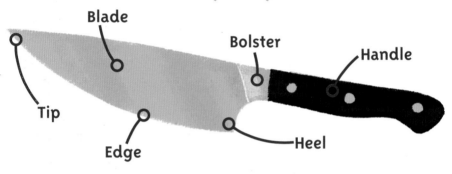

Blade

Bolster

Handle

Tip

Edge

Heel

If the knife is small, just grip it like you're giving it a firm handshake. *Hello, knife!* The handle should feel comfortable in your hand, not too big. If it's bigger (but still comfy for you), grip the handle with your thumb in front of the bolster on one side of the blade and your curved forefinger on the other side.

With your other hand, hold the food you're cutting with a flat side down so that it's steady. If the food doesn't have a flat side, ask an adult to help you cut a small piece off so that it does.

Grip the food by curving your fingers and thumb like claws so that your fingertips are curled away from the knife. Your knuckles will help keep your fingertips away from the sharp edge. This is called the claw grip.

When you cut, move the knife away from you and your fingers. Also, think low, and move the blade up and down only enough to get above your food.

Sharp Thinking

The more you know about knives, the safer you'll be. Here are the **Top 10 Things** to know when it comes to sharp edges.

1. Strange but true, sharp knives are safer knives. They are less likely to slip off the food, and you don't have to use as much pressure when you're cutting.

2. Make sure your hands and the knife handle are dry. Wet or oily = slippery = *whoops!*

3. Always cut on a cutting board made from wood or plastic. (Tip: To keep a cutting board from slipping, lay a damp towel under it.)

4. Don't touch the sharp edge of the blade. Even a light touch can mean there's a bandage in your future.

5. When you set a knife down, keep it away from the edge of the counter or table.

6. Don't struggle to cut something tough. Just put the knife down and ask an adult to do it.

7. Let a falling knife fall— don't try to catch it. Step away and warn others. *Look out!*

8. Don't put knives in bowls or sinks full of soapy water where you can't see them.

9. Use the right knife for the right job. A little paring knife won't do for a roast chicken.

10. The most important rule is this one: **Always have an adult nearby and watching when you use a knife.**

47

slicing & dicing

Chefs and recipes use some special terms for the different ways food can be cut.

Chop: to cut something into chunks or pieces. A recipe often gives you more information, such as, "Chop the pepper into 2-inch pieces." Or if the size doesn't matter so much, it might say "coarsely chop," which means bigger pieces, or "finely chop," which means smaller pieces.

Slice: to cut into thin sections.

Dice: to cut into small cubes—shaped like dice.

Julienne: to cut into thin strips.

Mince: to cut into teensy-weensy pieces.

Onions All Ways

You'll never bite into a big, juicy onion on its own. But chefs know that a bit of it makes savory dishes even more scrumptious. In your lifetime of cooking, you'll probably cut up thousands of them. Here's how.

Slice It

1. Carefully cut off a half-inch from the end of the onion that does *not* have a little clump of roots. Then set the onion on the flat end you just cut, and slice down from the top (where the root hairs are), cutting it in half. Peel off the top, papery layer from both halves.

2. Place one of the halves flat-side down on the cutting board, and hold it with the claw grip. With just the tip of your chef's knife touching the cutting board, move the heel of the blade down to slice off a thin half-circle shape from the end you first cut. Move your curved fingers back, scoot the knife over slightly, and slice again. Keep doing this until you have a pile of thin onion slices and there's not enough onion left at the root end to grip it safely.

3. Repeat step 2 with the other onion half. You can throw the root ends away.

Chop It

1. Repeat Slice It step 1 to get two peeled onion halves.

2. Hold one half of the onion using the claw grip, with the root end away from you, and slice it end to end (instead of side to side) into sections. The narrower the sections, the smaller the chopped pieces will be. Don't cut all the way through the hairy root. That end will hold the onion together.

3. Turn the onion and slice it side to side into thin sections, crosswise from the first cuts. The chopped pieces will simply fall away.

4. Repeat steps 2 and 3 with the other onion half. Throw away the onion's root end.

Mince It

Repeat steps 1–4 of Chop It.

5. Gather the chopped pieces into a compact pile. Put the tip of your knife on the far side of the pile, and place your free hand on top of the blade to keep the knife steady on the cutting board.

6. Rock the knife up and down, moving it back and forth across the pile, never letting the tip leave the cutting board. When the pile gets spread out, put the knife down and gather the bits into a pile again with your fingers. Then pick up the knife and continue cutting. Repeat until all of the onion is in tiny pieces.

peeling, grating & zesting

Knives aren't the only tools in the kitchen that cut food. Peelers remove skins from vegetables and fruits. Graters shred foods such as cheese into small bits. And a zester scrapes the tasty top layer off of fruits like oranges and lemons so it can lend its intense flavor to other foods.

A-Peeling Carrots

Wash the carrot under cold running water, and cut off the very tip of the pointed top. Holding the carrot at the thick end, start about halfway down and slide the peeler away from you, toward the tip, scraping off the thin skin. (Always peel away from your hand—the peeler blade is just like a knife.) Rotate the carrot slightly, and repeat until you've circled all the way around with the peeler. Then flip the carrot and peel the part that your hand was holding.

You can peel any long fruit or vegetable—such as a cucumber or a parsnip—this way.

A-Peeling Potatoes

Lumpy and curvy, potatoes are a little harder to peel than carrots. The method is basically the same, though. Wash the potato in cold water. Then hold it over a sink or bowl to catch the peels. Grasp it firmly at one end and peel away from your hand, turning it after each peel and flipping it to get the part your hand was covering. If little dark spots show up, peel the area a few extra times to cut them away. If a spot is deep, gently scoop it out with the tip of the peeler or have an adult help you cut it out with a small paring knife. You can peel any round veggie or fruit—such as a turnip or apple—this way.

Grate-er Cheese

To grate or shred a cheese such as cheddar or Parmesan, you need a grater. This might be a four-sided box grater with different-sized holes or a flat grater with a long handle. Larger holes are for shredding little strips, and smaller holes are for finer grating—such as the powdery Parmesan you sprinkle on spaghetti.

Hold the grater by the handle, pressing it down on a cutting board. Take a big chunk of cheese that is easy to hold, and press one side against the side of the grater. Keeping your fingertips and knuckles away from the metal (the edges of the holes are just like knives), slide the cheese down over the holes, so that the sharp edges slice off little bits and drop them into a pile. Stop when the chunk of cheese gets small or thin.

Zesty-Best Citrus

The zest is the thin, bright outer rind of a citrus fruit. When you zest a lemon or orange, you grate off that rind into tiny shreds. Zest has a strong flavor that livens up all kinds of foods, from muffins to pasta. It also makes a pretty garnish.

To zest a lemon or other citrus, you'll need a special kind of grater with very fine holes. A long, thin grating tool called a *microplane* works best. You can also use the smallest holes on a grater.

First, wash the fruit well with cool water and dry it. If you're using a microplane, hold the tool in the hand you use to write with, and hold the fruit in your other hand. Pull the microplane toward you over the fruit skin. Press firmly, but don't dig down into the white part underneath. That part—called the *pith*—tastes bitter.

If you're using a grater, follow the grating instructions on page 52.

When using either tool, keep the fingers that are holding the fruit out of the tool's way!

HOW TO

keeping it clean

Fruits & Veggies

You're pulling apart a head of lettuce for salad, and what do you see? *Dirt?* That's right. Lettuce grows in dirt. So do all fruits and veggies. And because they grew outside before coming into your kitchen, they have residues from such things as rainfall, birds and critters, and farm products. All fruits and vegetables need to be washed before you eat or cook with them, even if you're going to peel them.

Fruits & Veggies with Skins That You Eat

"Did you wash that apple?" How many times have you heard an adult say that? The list of fruits and veggies with edible outsides is long, and it includes apples, grapes, bell peppers, tomatoes, peaches, green beans, and cucumbers. Washing them is simple, though—and it doesn't involve soap. Just rub them gently while rinsing them under cool running tap water for 20 seconds or so.

Fruits and Veggies That You Peel or Cut Open

Carrots and potatoes, melons and oranges, and even bananas should be rinsed under cool running water before you peel or cut them. Why? Because this keeps any dirt and residues on the outside from getting on the yummy part that you're planning to eat.

Small & Delicate Berries

For strawberries, blueberries, raspberries, and blackberries, place them in a colander or strainer and rinse them under a gentle spray of cool tap water.

Lettuces, Spinach & Other Leafy Greens

First, separate the leaves. If they are large, tear them into smaller pieces. Place the leaves in the mesh basket of a salad spinner, inside the main bowl. Fill it with cold water and swish the leaves around. Lift out the mesh basket, empty the water, and repeat the whole rinsing process. Do this two or three times. Then pop the mesh basket back into the bowl, put the top on the spinner, and turn or press down on the handle to spin the leaves dry.

If you don't have a salad spinner, add the leaves to a bowl of cold, clean water. Swish them around, then lift them into a colander while you dump the water out of the bowl. Repeat two or three times. Then dry the leaves gently with paper towels.

Firm Veggies with Nooks & Crannies

Broccoli, cauliflower, and their cousins should be soaked in cold water for a couple of minutes before they get a final rinse under a cool faucet.

Meats

Raw meat—beef, pork, chicken, fish—is different from plant foods. It isn't dirty, exactly, but it naturally has germs that are killed when you cook it. It's an important job of the cook to make sure those germs—and any others—don't get spread to other food. The trick is to keep hands, tools, and cutting surfaces squeaky clean. Here's how.

DO wash your hands well with warm water and soap before you start cooking and after each time you handle raw foods such as meat or fresh eggs.

DO keep cold food cold, and hot food hot. If you're not using them right away, store fresh, uncooked foods in the refrigerator or freezer, making sure juices can't leak. Keep hot cooked foods in a spot that's warmer than 140 degrees.

DO wash tools, cutting boards, and counters after working with raw meat and before touching anything else, including other food.

DO cook food to the temperature the recipe calls for. Undercooked food can make you sick.

DO wash all your dishes and counters with hot water and soap. (Tip: Keep a bowl, tub, or sink full of soapy water standing by while you cook, so you can add dirty tools—except knives—to it as you go.)

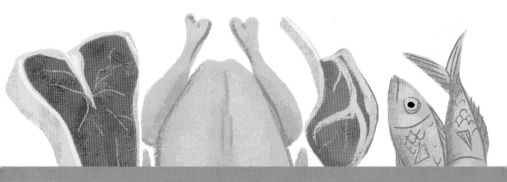

DON'T double dip. If you taste any food with a spoon or a potato chip, don't put that germy thing back into the food!

DON'T mix raw meat and its juices with other foods, and never put cooked meat back onto a plate or dish that held it when it was raw.

NO

DON'T lick a spoon or your fingers when you're handling food. "Finger-lickin' good" does not apply to cooking!

DON'T use the same cutting board for meats as you use for other foods. Try to use two boards, one for raw meat and the other for everything else. Wash the boards afterward in the dishwasher or with hot water and soap.

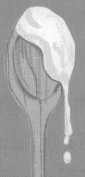

57

HOW TO

mixing it up

Stir it, beat it, fold it! Who knew there could be so many ways to combine ingredients?

Stir: to mix ingredients with a slow, smooth, circular motion until they're combined. Use a wooden spoon, fork, or the slow setting on a mixer (with adult help).

Beat: a fast mixing technique that takes stirring up a notch. Beating adds air to the mixture to make it smooth and light. By hand, use a wooden or other sturdy cooking spoon in a fast, circular motion. With an electric mixer, use a medium setting (and ask for an adult's help).

Whisk: an especially fast, energetic version of beating that pulls in a lot of air. Holding a whisk by its handle, whip it quickly back and forth in the mixture, then around and around, until the mixture gets thick and creamy or light and frothy. Or (with an adult) use a mixer on a high setting.

Tip

When you're mixing a batter or dough, don't overdo it. Too much mixing and handling can make a flour mixture tough and chewy when it's cooked. It's okay for batter to have a few lumps. They'll usually cook out.

Fold: to combine a light ingredient (such as whipped cream) with a heavier one (such as chocolate pudding) so that the light one stays light. Gently lift the heavier ingredient from underneath with a flexible rubber spatula, then fold it on top of the lighter one. Repeat until the two ingredients are barely mixed—and no more.

breaking it up

In cooking, you're actually *supposed* to break some things. Here are two ingredients that chefs break on a daily basis, plus the cracking and smashing techniques you'll need to know.

Cracking an Egg

It takes practice to crack an egg, but as you cook you'll get lots of that practice. Eggs are cooked in all kinds of dishes—and often you don't even know they're there, doing the job of adding a nice texture or holding ingredients together. (Of course, they can be yummy as the main event, too—like in an omelette or egg salad.)

Tap the egg sharply and firmly against the edge of a bowl. Aim for the middle of the egg. Then gently pull the shell apart from the bottom with your fingers, and let the egg yolk and white drop down into the bowl.

If you're adding an egg to other ingredients, crack it first into a separate small bowl. That way, you can scoop up any stray bits of shell before the egg goes into the mix.

Tip

To scoop up broken bits of eggshell, use another shell. Pieces of eggshell are attracted to each other.

Is It Rotten?

Eggs will stay fresh for at least five weeks in the fridge. If you're not sure whether an egg is still good, put it gently in a bowl of water. Fresh eggs will rest on the bottom. Rotten eggs will float, because air has seeped through their shells.

Smashing Garlic

A *head* of garlic—also called a *bulb*—is made up of many small sections called *cloves*, all packed together inside thin, papery skins. To break the head into individual cloves, place it pointy top down on a cutting board. Lean on it with the heel of your hand. The head will break up so that you can grab a clove or two.

Head

Clove

To peel the papery skin off a clove, set it on a cutting board, and carefully place the broad, flat side of a chef's knife on the clove, with the sharp edge facing away from you. Press on the side of the knife, and the skin will break away so that you can peel it off. At the same time, you can smash the garlic by pressing hard with the knife until the clove flattens. Set the knife aside, and pull off the skin. Your crushed garlic is now ready for that dish!

HOW To

What do pies, tarts, and shaped cookies all have in common beyond being tasty and beautiful? They all start with dough that needs to be rolled out thin and flat. It may take a bit of practice—but it's fun!

You'll need:

- Cookie or pastry dough, flattened into a round disk and chilled in the refrigerator
- Rolling pin
- Flour for "dusting"
- Large, flat work surface
- Pastry cloth or roll of wax paper

1. As always, wash your hands before you start.

2. Take the dough out of the refrigerator, and let it sit at room temperature for 5 to 10 minutes.

3. While that's happening, prepare your work surface. An ideal spot is the counter, because it's large and flat. Make sure the surface is clean. Then spread out a pastry cloth. If you don't have a cloth, tear off a sheet of wax paper about 15 inches long and use that instead. Sprinkle the cloth or paper with a light, even dusting of flour. The flour keeps the dough from sticking.

4. Put the disk of dough on your work surface, and lightly flour it on top. Dust your rolling pin with flour, too.

5. Holding the rolling pin by the ends, roll lightly but firmly across the dough, starting in the middle and rolling outward. Keep your pressure even, but ease up a little toward the edge of the dough so it's not thinner than the middle.

6. After every one or two rolls, rotate the dough by a quarter turn. Flour the work surface lightly each time under the dough so it doesn't stick. Also flour the top of the dough lightly if your rolling pin starts sticking. Your circle of dough will get larger and larger. Try to keep it as evenly round as possible. If your dough gets too warm and sticky while rolling, slide it onto a plate or baking sheet and put it back into the refrigerator for a few minutes to harden.

7. For cookies, stop when the dough is about ¼ to ½ inch thick. For pies, it should be about ⅛ to ¼ inch thick.

Cookies: Next Steps

1. Press your cookie cutter firmly into the dough. Metal cookie cutters without small details cut best and make cookies that are less likely to break.

2. Use a thin metal spatula to lift the cut cookie dough off the work surface and place it on a baking sheet. Space the cookies an inch apart.

Pie: Next Steps

1. Gently fold the floured dough in half, as if you're folding a piece of fabric. If it's sticking to your work surface, loosen it from beneath with a thin metal spatula. Lift it carefully, lay it down in the pie plate, and unfold it.

2. Press the dough into the sides of the plate, and trim off any large overhanging pieces with kitchen scissors.

3. Mark the top edge with a fork, pinch it into folds, or shape it any other way you like to make it neat or pretty.

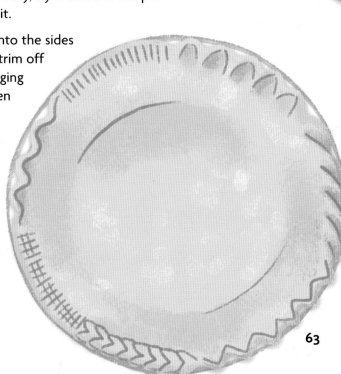

get
cracking!

ready, set, cook!

Q: What's the best way to learn to cook?

A: Just do it!

Begin with basic foods and easy recipes: pasta and rice, eggs and salads, roasts and veggies. When you know how to cook these standards, you can simply add ingredients or change a few steps to create your own custom meals.

Now is a good time to include your family and friends. You'll find out that every cook has her own way of doing things. Maybe your mom has a special way of hard boiling eggs. Maybe your best friend makes the best salad ever. Ask them! Try out their versions. Cooks form their own communities, and they love to trade ideas.

Fast Food?
It usually takes longer to make a dish than a recipe promises. Recipe writers can be optimistic. They assume the cook is experienced and wants to serve the food as fast as possible. Most cooks aren't like that, though. Just plan for more time— and have more fun!

Chef's Secret:
Putting in Place

Professional chefs cook fast because they follow a practice called *mise en place* *(meez on plahs)*, which is French for "put in place." They have all their ingredients prepped and ready to go before they start cooking. They chop all the foods that need chopping, mix all the sauces that need mixing, and set them out in separate dishes. You can do this, too. It may mean a few extra dishes to wash, but it makes things run much more smoothly. You'll cook like a pro!

hot terms

As a cook, you're a magician and heat is your magic wand. Add heat—and *poof!* Flour, sugar, and eggs transform into cookies. Potatoes turn into creamy mashes. Stiff, straight spaghetti becomes soft and twirlable.

Cooks divide heating techniques into two types: dry and moist. Dry methods use direct flames, or hot air, oil, or metal to cook food. Moist methods cook with hot liquids or steam.

Dry Heat Cooking

Bake: to cook on an uncovered pan in a heated oven. Although the term is often used specifically for bread or pastries, you can bake all kinds of foods, including mac and cheese, enchiladas, and lasagna. Baking browns the surface of food.

Roast: like baking, to cook food uncovered in a heated oven—but it usually refers to cooking meat or vegetables, often at a high temperature. Also like baking, roasting browns the food.

Broil: to cook food at very high heat, close to the flames or to the heating element in the top of your oven.

Grill: to use the high heat from an outdoor grill's flames to cook meat or veggies. Grilling and broiling both cook food quickly.

Fry: to cook in hot oil or butter on the stove top. Frying usually involves large pieces of food, such as chicken pieces, that are turned once or twice in the pan.

Sauté: like frying, except sautéing involves smaller pieces of food—such as chopped onion or mushrooms—that are stirred often. The word *sauté* means "jump" in French. (You might see the sizzling oil, or even the food, jump around in the skillet!)

Micro Magic

Unlike conventional ovens, which cook food by heating the air around it, microwave ovens actually make the food cook itself. A *magnetron* in the oven creates radio waves that bounce around and sink an inch or so into food, causing water, fat, and sugar molecules to flip back and forth. The moving molecules are hot, so *abracadabra!*—their own heat cooks the food.

Moist Heat Cooking

Boil: to cook in water or another liquid that's been heated until its surface bubbles. A *rolling boil* or *rapid boil* is when the bubbles are so energetic you can't quiet them down by stirring them. (Tip: You can bring a pot of water to a boil faster if you cover it with a lid.)

Simmer: to cook in a pot of liquid that's almost boiling. Simmering water will have small, occasional bubbles but won't reach a full boil.

Poach: to cook gently by just barely covering the food with water (or another liquid) kept below the boiling point. Eggs and fish are often cooked this way.

Braise: to cook food—usually large pieces of meat—partly covered by liquid in a covered pot. It's a slow method that's especially well suited for cuts of meat that would be tough if cooked another way.

Steam: to cook food such as vegetables or fish in a covered pot or dish using—you guessed it—steam. A steamer basket is often used to hold the food above the steaming liquid.

Hot Safety Tips

Heat's hot! It cooks, but it can go too far and burn. Here are 12 **Top Tips** for handling hot stuff:

1. Before you use them, know how to turn stoves, ovens, and microwaves on and off and how to control their temperatures.

2. If you're using gas burners on a stove, look for a flame when they're turned on. Sometimes on low heat they give off gas but don't light up. This can be dangerous. Usually you can smell the gas; it has a distinctive odor. If this happens, turn off the burner and tell an adult right away.

3. Remember that stove tops can stay hot after you've turned them off, even if they look dark or cool. Ovens, too, can get hot on the outside. Don't lean against them.

4. Never, ever, ever leave cooking food unattended.

5. Always use oven mitts (which fit over your hands) or pot holders (which are flat squares) to pick up anything from a hot stove top, oven, or microwave. If you're not sure whether something is hot, use them anyway. Check them for worn-out or wet spots, which will let heat come through.

6. Keep pot handles turned away from the edges of stove tops or counters so they don't get knocked over—or grabbed by little brothers and sisters! Make sure the handles aren't over an open flame or hot burner either.

7. When you're lifting the lid of a hot pot to check what's inside, lift the side that's away from your face. That way you won't get a face full of hot steam.

8. Full pots and pans can be very heavy. Ask an adult to move them for you—don't try to do it yourself. Also have an adult move any pan with hot liquid in it, no matter its size.

9. Keep your hands and face back from hot, bubbling liquids in pots and skillets. Use oven mitts and a long-handled spoon or spatula when you stir.

10. Ask an adult when you need to drop something such as pasta or corn on the cob into hot water. Hot water can splash!

11. If something in a pot or pan catches fire, yell immediately! Don't try to move the pan. Never pour water on a kitchen fire—water can actually spread an oily fire instead of putting it out. An adult might be able to put out a small pan fire by pouring baking soda on it or by putting a lid over the pan.

12. If you burn yourself, alert an adult immediately! Very minor burns can be soothed under cold running water for a couple of minutes.

how to read a recipe

A recipe gives you step-by-step directions for cooking a dish, along with all the ingredients you'll need. Think of a recipe as the voice of the original cook talking directly to you.

The top trick for making a dish turn out well is this:

Read through the whole recipe, from start to finish, before you begin cooking.

You'll have a clear idea of what you'll need to do and how long each step will take, so you can avoid surprises.

How many people this recipe will feed (If you want to feed more or fewer people, you'll need to adjust all the ingredients accordingly.)

All the items you need for the recipe, often in the order you'll use them (This list may tell you how to prepare each ingredient before you get to the directions.)

Step-by-step instructions (These should be very exact and give the time it takes to do each task.)

quesadilla

 Ask an adult to help with the knives, grater, and stove.

Ingredients:

Vegetable-oil spray

Flour tortillas
4 medium (8-inch)

Cheddar, Jack, or mozzarella cheese
grated, 1 cup

Fresh or frozen cooked vegetables
such as corn, black beans, or chopped scallions, 1 cup total

Toppings (optional)
such as guacamole, salsa, or sour cream

Directions:

1. Set a large skillet or griddle on the stove and coat it with vegetable-oil spray. Place a tortilla in the pan. Sprinkle the cheese and vegetables onto the tortilla. Cover with the second tortilla.

2. Turn on the burner to medium. Check the quesadilla as it cooks by lifting one side with a spatula and peeking underneath. The tortilla will get toasty brown with nice brown spots, and the cheese will melt. Cook for 3 to 5 minutes.

3. Flip the quesadilla with the spatula.

4. Cook the second side for about 2 minutes until it is also toasty brown. Use the spatula to move the quesadilla to a cutting board.

5. Let the quesadilla cool for a couple of minutes, and then cut it into quarters. Eat it plain—yum!—or topped with condiments such as guacamole, salsa, or sour cream.

easy eggs

Eggs are practically the perfect food. Full of protein to build your muscles, they're also easy to cook. Scrambled, they make a quick breakfast. Deviled, they're a delight for parties.

simple scramble

makes 2 servings

 Ask an adult to help with the stove.

Ingredients:

Butter 1 tablespoon

Eggs 4 medium or large

Salt ½ teaspoon

Milk 1 tablespoon

Directions:

1. Crack the eggs into a medium-size bowl, and whisk them until the whites and yolks blend together. Add the salt.

2. Put a medium skillet on the stove. Add the butter. Turn on the burner to medium heat. Keep an eye on the butter as it melts.

3. As soon as the butter is melted, turn the heat down to medium-low and pour the eggs into the skillet. Stir them with a wooden spoon or plastic spatula. Push them around as they cook, about 2 to 3 minutes. As soon as they are solid, turn off the heat. Immediately scrape the eggs onto two plates and serve.

Options:

• For cheesy eggs, stir in ½ cup grated cheddar or Jack cheese after adding the eggs to the skillet.

• For spicy eggs, top the cooked eggs with 1 tablespoon of your favorite salsa.

devilish delights

 Ask an adult to help with the knives, stove, and boiling water.

Ingredients:

Hard-boiled eggs
4 medium or large

Mayonnaise
2 tablespoons

Prepared mustard
½ teaspoon

Salt ½ teaspoon

Paprika sprinkle

Directions:

1. Cut each peeled, hard-boiled egg in half lengthwise. Over a medium-size bowl, pop out the yolks by gently squeezing the egg with your fingers. Set the hollowed-out egg whites on a plate.

2. With a fork, mash the egg yolks in the bowl with the mayonnaise, mustard, and salt.

3. With a small spoon, scoop up the egg yolk mixture and press one scoopful into each hollowed-out egg half.

4. Sprinkle paprika across the top of each.

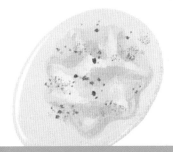

Hard-Boiled Know-How

1. Gently lay the eggs in a saucepan, and fill with cold water to an inch or two above the eggs.

2. Put the pan on the stove. Turn on the burner to medium-high heat.

3. As soon as the water starts to boil, turn off the heat and cover the saucepan with a tight-fitting lid. Set the timer for 15 minutes.

4. After the timer sounds, use a slotted spoon to move the cooked eggs out of the pan to a bowl of cold water. When cool, roll an egg on a cutting board until its shell cracks all over. Then peel it over the bowl, rinsing it until the shell is gone.

Tip: If you live in the mountains, set the timer for 18 to 20 minutes. At high altitudes (above 3,500 feet), water boils at a lower temperature, so foods take longer to cook.

fruit smoothies

Smoothies are smashing as a quick breakfast or an afternoon snack. Bananas are part of many smoothie recipes, because they add sweetness and a creamy texture. Very ripe bananas—the ones with brown spots—are best!

banana classic

makes 1 smoothie

 Ask an adult to help with the knives and blender.

Ingredients:

Bananas 2 whole ripe

Milk 1 cup

Honey 2 teaspoons

Ice cubes 3

Directions:

1. Peel the bananas and break them into chunks. (For **variations**, prepare your other fruits.)

2. Put all the ingredients into the blender container.

3. Put the lid on tight, hold it down with your hand, and start the blender on a slow speed.

4. After about 10 seconds, turn the speed to high and blend until the liquid is smooth, with no large chunks.

5. Turn off the blender, pour the smoothie into a tall glass, and drink it right away.

variations

The possibilities are endless. Try these, or make up your own, using your favorite fruits, yogurts, and juices. Just follow the directions for the Banana Classic.

Berry-Yogurt Smoothie

Frozen berries take the place of ice cubes in this colorful variation.

Ingredients:

Banana 1 ripe, peeled and broken into chunks

Berries 1 cup frozen

Plain or vanilla yogurt ½ cup

Orange juice ½ cup

No-Dairy Apple Smoothie

Use almond or soy milk in smoothies if you're avoiding dairy products.

Ingredients:

Banana ½ ripe, peeled and broken into chunks

Apple 1 small, cored, peeled, and chopped into a few pieces

Unsweetened vanilla almond milk ¾ cup

Honey 1 teaspoon

Cinnamon ¼ teaspoon

Ice cube 1

Mango Lassi

Traditional in India, Pakistan, and Bangladesh, lassis are the original smoothie!

Ingredients:

Mango 1½ cups frozen chunks

Plain yogurt 1½ cups

Orange juice ½ cup

Honey 2 tablespoons

Ice cubes 4

great basics

Rice and pasta are some of the simplest foods to cook. You can make them in different ways, but boiling is easiest. With rice, you use just enough water for the rice to absorb. With pasta, fill your pot with lots of water and let the pasta swim.

ready rice

makes 4 servings

 Ask an adult to help with the stove, boiling water, and knives.

Ingredients:

Long-grain white rice
uncooked, 1 cup

Water 2 cups

Salt ½ teaspoon

Hot or Not?

Starting with hot tap water might get your pot to a boil faster, but it could be bad for your health. Hot water can dissolve traces of minerals and metals as it flows through the pipes in your house. For this reason, it's best to cook with and drink only from the cold tap.

Directions:

1. Put the uncooked rice in a medium-size saucepan. Add water and salt.

2. Put the pan on the stove, uncovered, and turn on the burner to medium-high heat. When the water reaches a rolling boil, turn the heat down to low and cover the pot.

3. Set the timer and simmer the rice for 16 to 18 minutes, until it's tender and all the water has been absorbed.

4. Turn off the heat, move the pot to a cold burner, and let the rice sit for another 5 minutes, covered, to steam a bit more.

5. Fluff it with a fork and serve.

Options:

• Use 2 cups chicken broth or stock instead of water for more flavor.

• Stir ¼ cup chopped fresh parsley, 1 tablespoon lemon juice, and 1 tablespoon butter into the cooked rice for a delicious side dish.

perfect pasta

 Ask an adult to help with the large pot, stove, boiling water, and grater.

Ingredients:

Spaghetti
uncooked, 1 pound

Salt 2 teaspoons

Directions:

1. Fill a large, deep pot about three quarters full of cold water, add the salt, and put it on the stove.

2. Turn the burner to medium-high heat. Bring the water to a rolling boil.

3. Carefully add the pasta to the boiling water. (Don't splash yourself!) Cook it, uncovered, at a medium boil. As the pasta begins to soften, push it under the water and stir it often with a long-handled spoon or pasta fork. If you don't, it can clump together or stick to the bottom of the pot.

4. Set a colander in the sink.

5. Cook the pasta as long as the package says, usually 9 to 12 minutes for spaghetti. (Have an adult lift out a strand or two to test.) The pasta should be tender but not mushy.

6. Ask an adult to drain the pasta into the colander in the sink. Then transfer the pasta to a large bowl.

Options:

• For a simple but tasty sauce, stir 3 tablespoons of olive oil into the pasta. Let it cool for at least 5 minutes. Then add ⅓ cup grated Parmesan cheese. If the pasta is warm but not hot, the cheese will make a sauce with the oil. (If it's too hot, the cheese will melt into a clump.)

• For a tangy flavor, add to the cooked spaghetti 2 tablespoons olive oil, ½ cup pitted Kalamata olives, and ⅔ cup oil-packed sun-dried tomatoes, drained.

79

beautiful bird

A roasted chicken is easy and delicious—and it makes an impressive centerpiece for a great family dinner!

roast chicken

makes 4 servings

★ Ask an adult to help with the knives, the oven, a meat thermometer, and handling raw chicken.

Ingredients:

Whole chicken 3½ to 4 pounds

Lemon 1 medium

Olive oil 1 tablespoon

Salt ½ teaspoon

Ground black pepper ½ teaspoon

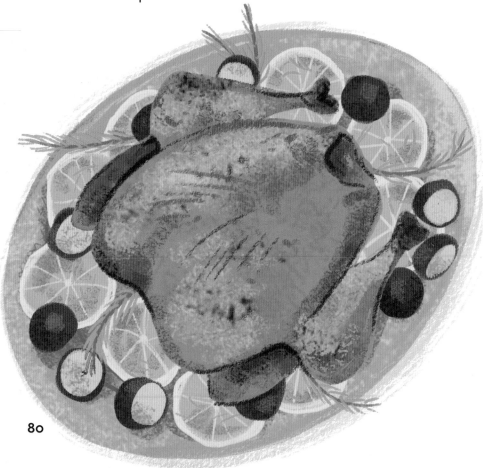

Directions:

1. Heat the oven to 425 degrees.

2. Prepare the ingredients and tools so that you don't have to touch anything in the kitchen while you're handling the raw chicken. Slice the lemon in half crosswise. Measure the olive oil into a small bowl, and the salt and pepper into another small bowl. Set all ingredients near the sink. Tear several paper towels off a roll and place them with your prepared ingredients. Place a rack in a roasting pan and set it nearby, too.

3. Place the raw chicken in a clean sink, and pull out the giblets. Giblets are pieces such as the chicken neck and liver, wrapped in paper and stuffed into the chicken's opening. You won't use them for the roast chicken, so ask an adult what he or she wants to do with them.

4. Stuff the lemon halves into the chicken's opening. They'll give the bird a nice lemony smell when it cooks and help keep it moist.

5. Dry the chicken all over with the paper towels. Then drizzle the olive oil over it and rub the oil into the skin. Sprinkle the salt and pepper over the skin.

6. Place the chicken on the rack in the pan, breast side up.

7. Now have an adult turn on the faucet so you don't get chicken juices on it. Wash your hands with soap and warm water, and keep washing until you've sung "Happy Birthday" two times through.

8. Slide the roasting pan into the oven on the center rack. Set a timer for 55 minutes. If the chicken looks brown and juicy when the timer goes off, insert a meat thermometer deep into the thigh but without touching the bone. If it reads 165 degrees, it's time to remove the chicken from the oven. If it's less than 165 degrees, put it back in the oven for 5 to 10 minutes and take the temperature again.

9. When it's 165 degrees, it's done. Let the chicken sit for 10 minutes. Then it's ready to carve, serve—and enjoy!

Options:

Add root vegetables to the pan about 20 minutes after you put the chicken in the oven. Try peeled carrots or peeled parsnips cut into 1-inch pieces, small red potatoes that are washed but unpeeled, or Brussels sprouts. Lightly coat them with vegetable-oil spray before they go in the oven.

fish feast

A delish fish dish is a must-have for a chef's recipe file. When small tomatoes roast in the oven with the fish, they turn sweet and juicy, making a tangy sauce.

saucy salmon

makes 4 servings

Ask an adult to help with the knives, the oven, handling raw fish, and checking the fish to make sure it's done.

Ingredients:

Salmon filets with or without skin, about 1½ pounds

Cherry or grape tomatoes about 15 whole

Parsley fresh, 2 tablespoons

Garlic cloves 3 medium

Canola oil 3 tablespoons

Lemons 3 medium

Dijon mustard 2 teaspoons

Salt ¼ teaspoon

Ground black pepper pinch

Directions:

1. Heat the oven to 425 degrees.

2. Line a baking sheet with aluminum foil. (This will make clean-up much easier.) A baking sheet with shallow sides will work best.

3. Prepare all of your ingredients so that you don't have to touch anything in the kitchen while you're handling raw fish. Wash the tomatoes, pat them dry with a paper towel, and set them aside in a clean bowl. Wash, pat dry, and chop the parsley. Peel and mince the garlic cloves. Cut 1 lemon cross-wise and squeeze to get 3 tablespoons of juice; cut an additional lemon if needed. Cut lemon slices from a new lemon to be used for decoration, and set them aside.

4. Whisk the oil, squeezed lemon juice, and mustard together in a medium bowl until the mixture is creamy. Add the parsley, garlic, salt, and pepper, and stir with a spoon to mix.

5. If it's not already cut, divide the salmon into 4 portions about the same size and thickness, and place them on the baking sheet—skin-side down, if there's skin.

6. Now wash your hands with soap and warm water. Keep washing until you've sung "Happy Birthday" two times through. Have an adult turn on the faucet for you so that you don't get fish juice on it.

7. Add the tomatoes to the sauce in the bowl and coat them gently, using a spoon. With the spoon, lift out the tomatoes and spread them around the baking sheet between the fish slices. Then spread the remaining sauce on the top and sides of the fish. Last, top each piece of fish with a lemon slice.

8. Slide the baking sheet into the oven on the center rack. Set the timer for 12 minutes.

9. When the timer sounds, take the fish out of the oven and check it to make sure it's just cooked through. It should be light pink, with a slightly darker pink center, and should flake when poked with a fork.

10. Arrange the fish and tomatoes on plates or a platter. Use a spatula to gently lift the food piece by piece from the sheet.

Options:
Try the recipe with a different fish, such as tilapia or halibut. If the fish is thinner than salmon, like tilapia, check it at 10 minutes. If it's thick, such as a halibut steak, check it at 15 minutes.

gorgeous greens

Crisp, cool, and colorful salads are the perfect side for just about any meal, including spaghetti, roast chicken, a burger, soup, and mac and cheese.

super simple salad

makes 4 servings

 Ask an adult to help with the knives.

Ingredients:

Lettuce and other leafy greens 4–6 cups total

Cherry tomatoes 1 pint (or less)

Feta cheese ½ cup crumbled

Start with lettuces. Combine two or three kinds, if you can, mixing crispy leaves with soft ones, dark greens with bright lime and deep purple colors, and mild tastes with sharp notes. You can buy different greens already mixed in a bag, or choose your own favorites at the store. A simple "just the leaves" salad is elegant and yummy, but you can also add other favorite veggies for even more color and variety.

Directions:

1. Prepare the greens by washing them (see page 55) and tearing them into bite-size pieces. With an adult's help, slice the tomatoes in half.

2. Place all the ingredients in a large salad bowl.

3. Just before serving, drizzle ⅓ cup salad dressing (see page 85) over the salad; then toss it with salad tossers or large spoons to coat the leaves.

Options:

• Add ¼ cup sliced cucumber, ¼ cup pitted black olives, and ¼ sliced red onion for a Greek flavor.

• Instead of tomatoes and cheese, add apple slices and ¼ cup walnut halves.

salad dressing

Whisk together oil and vinegar to create an easy and delicious basic called a *vinaigrette (vihn-ih-gret)*.

makes enough dressing for 4 servings of salad

Ingredients:

Extra-virgin olive oil
6 tablespoons

Vinegar—white wine,
red wine, or sherry
3 tablespoons

Salt ¼ teaspoon

Ground black
pepper pinch

Directions:

1. Combine all ingredients in a small bowl.

2. Using a whisk, mix briskly until the oil and vinegar form a creamy-looking dressing. (If you don't use the dressing right away, the oil and vinegar will separate. If that happens, just whisk it again.)

Options:

- Add 1 teaspoon honey for a sweeter taste.

- Add 1 teaspoon Dijon mustard for a sharper taste.

Why Whisk?

You've heard the saying, "Oil and water don't mix." It's true. Water drops like to be with other water drops, and oil clings to oil. Vinegar is mostly water, so oil-and-vinegar dressings separate into a layer of vinegar floating on top of the oil, unless you whisk them really well or shake them in a closed jar. Then they blend—but only for a while. Soon they separate again. You can add an *emulsifier* to help them stick together longer. Mustard and fresh garlic are ideal emulsifiers because they taste great in a salad dressing!

veggies two ways

With their many colors and textures, vegetables are ideal side dishes. Stir-fry them for quick and colorful crunch, or steam them for a simple side to a saucy main dish.

broccoli stir-fry

makes 4 servings

 Ask an adult to help with the knives and the stove.

Ingredients:

Canola oil
1 or 2 tablespoons

Red pepper flakes
⅛ teaspoon

Broccoli florets 2 cups

Garlic 1 clove

Salt pinch

Directions:

1. Prepare the vegetables: Peel and mince the garlic. Wash the broccoli and cut it into large pieces (1 to 2 inches).

2. Add the oil to the skillet, using 1 tablespoon if the skillet is nonstick or 2 tablespoons if it's not.

3. Add the red pepper flakes to the skillet.

4. Heat the oil over medium-high heat.

5. When the oil is hot, add the broccoli and garlic to the pan.

6. Stir the vegetables constantly for about 4 minutes, until they are tender but still crisp. The broccoli should be bright green.

7. Turn off the heat, sprinkle on the salt, and serve the veggies immediately.

Options:

- Many vegetables can be stir-fried, alone or together, including green beans, bell peppers of all colors, yellow squash, and zucchini. Chop them into 1-inch chunks or ½-inch slices.

- For richer flavor, add ½ cup chopped or thinly sliced onion when you start cooking the veggies.

steamed green beans

 Ask an adult to help with the stove, boiling water, and steam.

Ingredients:

Green beans ½ pound

Butter 1 teaspoon

Salt ¼ teaspoon

Ground black pepper pinch

Directions:

1. Wash the green beans. Snap off the ends using your fingers.

2. Add water to a medium saucepan, about 1 inch deep, and place a steamer basket inside.

3. Add the beans to the basket in an even layer.

4. Put the pan on the stove, cover with a well-fitting lid, and turn the burner on high.

5. Once the water starts boiling, lower the heat to medium and let the vegetables steam for about 4 minutes.

6. Empty the cooked beans into a small serving bowl and top with butter, salt, and pepper. Serve while they are still hot.

Options:

• If you don't have a steamer basket, use a straight-sided skillet (with a lid) that contains ½ inch of water and the salt. Bring the water to a boil before adding the beans; then cover and cook for 4 minutes.

• Asparagus and cauliflower florets are great for steaming, and they take about the same amount of time. Snap off the woody ends of the asparagus using your fingers.

sweet treats

What's better than a sweet, juicy strawberry? A sweet, juicy strawberry plus chocolate! Chocolate-dipped strawberries make an excellent dessert or party snack. Ask some friends to help—it's fun to do together!

chocolate-dipped strawberries

makes about 20 strawberries

Ask an adult to help with the microwave and hot chocolate.

The key to getting a good chocolate coating is to make sure the strawberries are completely dry. Even a little water will make the chocolate grainy, and it won't stick as well.

Ingredients:

Strawberries fresh, 1 pound

Dark or semisweet chocolate chips 12-ounce package

Directions:

1. Gently wash the strawberries in a colander under cold running water. Then carefully dry the berries with a paper towel. Let them sit on a clean, dry towel to finish drying off, about 15 to 30 minutes.

2. Line a large baking sheet with wax paper or parchment paper.

3. Pour the chocolate chips into a microwave-safe bowl, and heat them on the defrost setting in the microwave for 30 seconds. Take the bowl out of the microwave and stir the chocolate with a wooden spoon or rubber spatula. If the chips are not completely melted, put them back in the microwave for another 30 seconds. Repeat until the chocolate is liquid and smooth. (Note: Chocolate can get quite hot in the microwave. Don't stick your finger in it!)

4. Pick up each strawberry by its leafy stem and dip it in the chocolate until it's about ⅔ covered. Twirl it to let any extra chocolate drip off. Then place it on the baking sheet.

5. When all the strawberries are covered, let them sit on a counter or in the fridge until the chocolate covering is hard, about 30 minutes. Eat them within one day—which shouldn't be hard!

Options:
• Use clementine sections instead of strawberries.

• Scatter candy sprinkles over the chocolate coating while it's still wet.

cooking 911: help for kitchen emergencies

Q: Yuck! My soup is way too salty. What do I do?

A: You can't take salt out of a soup, but you can add more soup to the salt. If you have any broth or stock left over, add about ½ cup at a time—or use water. Taste the soup after each addition until the saltiness is just right.

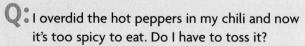

Q: Oh, no! The cookies are burned on the bottom. Can they be saved?

A: Probably. If they're burned only on the bottom but are otherwise okay, gently scrape off the burned parts with a zester or a grater with very small holes.

Q: I overdid the hot peppers in my chili and now it's too spicy to eat. Do I have to toss it?

A: Not at all. Dairy foods—such as milk, yogurt, or sour cream—are the enemies of *capsaicin*, the spicy oil in hot peppers. Add a few table-spoons of yogurt or sour cream to your chili bowl, and you'll turn down the heat.

Q: The brown sugar is hard as a rock. How can I make my cookies?

A: Brown sugar gets hard if it dries out, but the answer is as close as your microwave oven. Put the sugar in a microwave-safe bowl, set a damp (not wet) paper towel on top of the sugar, and cover the bowl with plastic wrap. Microwave about 10 seconds at a time, testing until the sugar is soft.

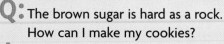

Q: My freshly baked cake is stuck to the pan. How can I unstick it?

A: If you have at least 6 hours to spare, let the cake cool and pop it in the freezer, covered by plastic wrap. After 6 hours, take it out, run a table knife around all the edges to loosen it, then use two spatulas on opposite sides to lift the frozen cake from the pan. If you're short on time, let the cake cool and then lower the pan into a larger roasting pan that's holding an inch or so of hot water. The heat should loosen the bottom. Remove it in the same way as above, but be careful: A warm cake is more likely to crumble than a frozen one.

Q: Okay, I did that and a piece broke off my cake. Now what?

A: Don't panic! That's what frosting is for. Use a bit of your frosting as glue to stick the pieces together. If the cake is too broken up, cut it into pieces, drizzle chocolate syrup over it, add whipped cream, and call it a triumph.

Q: The vegetables are an overcooked, mushy mess. What can I do?

A: Add a little butter and a pinch of salt, and mash them with a potato masher or (with adult help) a blender. Now you have an elegant vegetable puree.

Q: Aargh! I spilled cooking oil all over the counter. There's too much just to wipe clean. How can I fix this?

A: Flour to the rescue! With an adult's permission, pour a cup or two of white flour over the oil. Let it soak up the oil into a damp lump, scoop the lump into a dustpan or plate, and throw it away. Then you can finish with a cleaning spray and paper towel.

it happened to me!

My friend and I were making a cake. I added eggs and oil, and then *she* added eggs and oil. We didn't see each other do it! That was a wacky cake!

—AG Fan

When I was baking cookies with my sister, I accidentally turned the mixer on the highest setting. Flour went everywhere! Our kitchen looked like the North Pole.

—AG Fan

One time I made a coffee cake and read the directions wrong. They called for ⅔ cup of water, and I thought that meant 2 or 3 cups. It was a very watery cake.

—Megan

One time I was rushing and trying to make brownies quickly. I started making them and then realized I didn't have eggs or flour. Always make sure you have all the ingredients before you start.

—Emilia

My sister and I were baking lemon cookies. The recipe called for half a tablespoon of lemon juice. We accidentally put in half a cup. Sour!!!

—AG Fan

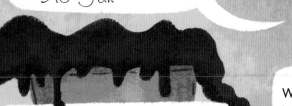

My dad and I were baking a cake, and instead of filling the pan halfway, we filled it all the way. The cake overflowed in the oven. What a mess!

—Sophia

When my sister was little, she got her hair tangled in the mixer! (Her hair was long.)

—Maya

My friend and I wanted to make a giant cookie. We mixed the dough and put it on a pizza pan with no sides. It melted over the sides and all over in the oven! We won't be trying that again.

—Rachel

I realized our baking powder was 12 years old, but I used it anyway. The cookies didn't puff up at all!

—Cosway

Do NOT forget to put the top on your blender!!!

—Grace

We were making muffins and forgot to put in baking powder. They were flat, and they tasted really bad.

—Michele

I don't know how this happened, but we added salt instead of sugar to our cake. Yuck!!

—Zoe

I made chocolate chip cookies, and they looked perfect! Then I bit into one, and it was hard as stone. It turns out I measured the flour wrong.

—Sarah

I was cooking garlic and onions but went to help my mom and forgot. They burned!

—Gianna

from soup
to nuts

thinking ahead

You know what a whisk is. You know how to slice and how to dice. You understand the what and why of food groups. You even know how to roast a whole chicken. It's time to put it all together.

For good cooks, the first step in planning a meal doesn't happen in the kitchen. It happens before that, in your mind, when you're imagining the dishes you'll serve. This is the time to remember **happy & healthy.**

Tastes sooo yummy

Looks de-LISH

Easy for me to cook— I can do this!

Fun to serve—they will love it!

Fruits—*check!*

Veggies—*check!*

Protein—*check!*

Dairy or calcium—*check!*

Grains—*check!*

Mashed potatoes, rice pilaf, and French bread are truly scrumptious. But you probably know that a dinner plate with only these foods wouldn't score high on the Healthy Test. It might surprise you, though, that it wouldn't score high on the Happy Test either, because it doesn't have much of that spice of life called variety. The best meals are a creative combo of elements that appeal to all the different senses.

Colors

Vegetables, fruits, and herbs are an artist's color palette for sides, salads, and sauces.

Textures

Chunky salads and stir-fry. Chewy pasta. Light lettuces. Moist, succulent meats and fish. Crispy, crunchy crusts and toppings. Creamy mashes and sauces. Each food can make a delicious statement with the way it feels.

Tip

Smaller servings look yummier on a plate than large servings.

Shapes & Sizes

Large and small. Round, thin, long, square. Flat or mounded or puddled. It's easy to present a pleasing visual variety of shapes and sizes with foods from any group.

Flavors

Savory or sweet. Spicy or cooling. Strong or mellow. Tangy or earthy or buttery. Chefs think of flavors like musical notes in a song. Too many and they can clash, but a few well-chosen ones create a happy harmony.

Temperatures

Not everything has to be hot out of the oven! A cooling salsa, cheese at room temperature, or fresh greens from the fridge or garden add many more "degrees" of variety.

the five senses of cooking

Cooking is one of the few activities that truly use all five senses.

Vision

Your eyes often tell you when food is ready or not. Is the cheese on that pizza bubbling and golden brown? Are the muffins puffing high over the tins? Are those sautéed beans bright green? More than that, the sight of a colorful fruit salad or a beautiful iced cake is pure pleasure.

Hearing

Your ears tell you more than you might think. The sound of boiling water alerts you that it's time to add the pasta. The sizzling of a steak is saying, "Check me!" That plopping sound on the stove means it's time to stir the sauce. DING! Something is ready to come out of the oven!

Taste

That's obvious!

Smell

Without a sense of smell, you don't actually have much of a sense of taste. It's your nose that tells the difference between a banana and a mango, or cinnamon and pepper. And just think how happy you feel when the scent of baking cookies or simmering spaghetti sauce wafts through the house. "Oooh, what's that smell?"

Touch

You gently press the top of a cake to see if it rises back up. You wiggle a chicken leg to see if it's loose and fully cooked. Is it cool enough or warm enough to be just right?

mind over menus

You're thinking like an artist. Your creative imagination is turned on high, and you've got hundreds of ideas to try. But how do you choose which ones to put on the plate? Here are some practical pointers that chefs follow when they organize their ideas into smart menus.

Think in Threes

For most meals, three is the ideal number of foods—each from a different food group. Want a quick breakfast? Go for cereal, blueberries, and milk in one handy bowl. For lunch, maybe a sandwich with meat and lettuce, a yogurt, and an apple. If it's dinner, combine a main dish such as roast chicken with a vegetable side dish and a grain.

If your main dish is already a combo of several foods, though, just one side is fine. If you're serving a bean chili or chicken vegetable soup, for example, think crusty bread to fill the missing grain slot. Lasagna or mac and cheese? A big green salad easily completes the picture.

Remember Food Preferences

Are you feeding vegetarians? People with allergies? Friends with food traditions? The chef's job is not only to make the meal. You're also a host, and you want everyone at your table to feel welcome.

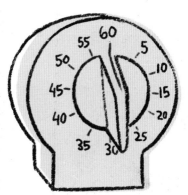

Consider the Clock

To avoid juggling all of your dishes at the last minute, try to make some foods or do some prep in advance. Or you could have one dish in the oven while you work on another. And ask for help—not just from the adult who's in the kitchen with you. When more friends and family pitch in, you multiply the fun!

recipe finds

Getting ready to plan a family feast? Looking for lunchbox ideas?
Weary of the same smoothie you've been sipping since September?
Recipes are everywhere, if you know where to find them.

Family & Friends

What was that amazing cheesy crunchy spicy pepper noodle thing your Aunt Erin brought for dinner last Halloween? And those scones at Neesha's slumber party—you can't get them off your mind! Think of family traditions and new discoveries with friends, and ask for the recipe. Cooks love it when you love their food, and they usually love to share.

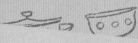

Cookbooks

Cookbooks for new cooks. Cookbooks with just desserts, or just pizza, or just salads. Cookbooks with foods from around the world—India, France, China, Mexico, Greece, Thailand. Cookbooks for vegetarians, vegans, and cheese lovers. Whatever your food passion, there's a cookbook to satisfy it. Visit the library and bring home a stack!

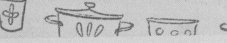

Magazines

Many magazines offer new recipes in every issue. Some magazines are all about food, cover to cover. Some are especially for kids—and some are aimed at adults, but you can follow that "Truly Tempting Tacos" recipe as well as your parents can. See what's around your house. Check out the magazines in the grocery store. Look in the newspaper. Recipes are everywhere!

Websites & Apps

Surf's up! A whole world of recipes is at your fingertips. Ask an app or the Internet for "recipes," and you're likely to get millions! So be more specific. Looking for something special to do with burgers? Type "burger recipes." A new take on pumpkin pie for Thanksgiving? Type "pumpkin pie recipes." Do you have an ingredient that you need to use? Type "rhubarb recipes" or "chocolate chip recipes"—you're bound to find a winner.

Cooking Shows

On TV there are shows and even whole networks devoted to chefs, food, and cooking competitions. They're fun to watch, but keep them in perspective. Cooking for real people isn't supposed to be a contest. Food doesn't have to be fancy or made with ingredients you've never heard of. Cooking is about making and sharing food that's good for the body and makes people happy. It's as simple as that.

the lunchbox

There's no need to worry about mystery meat or pretend pizza when you pack your own lunch. Just follow a few guidelines, and when cafeteria time rolls around, you'll be living large on your own creations.

Look for new sandwich ideas, and cycle through your standards, too. Try different breads: pita pocket, spinach wrap, French baguette, English muffin, whole wheat raisin bread. Combine nut butters with fruits. With sliced meats, add a slice of cheese and a handful of greens for punch and crunch. Make a veggie sandwich from carrots, cucumber, and hummus. The varieties are endless!

An insulated lunchbag or lunchbox is best.

Pack favorite dinner leftovers in a vacuum container that keeps food safely hot for up to 8 hours. Don't forget the spoon!

Pack wet items such as sliced tomatoes or strawberries in their own containers so you don't end up with soggy bread or salad.

Include fresh fruits and vegetables. They're colorful, easy, healthy, and, yes, yummy—especially if you have a little salad dressing or peanut butter for dip.

Make sure your bags and containers are closed. You've been dreaming about your lunch since second period. The last thing you want is to find it spilled in the bottom of your box.

Freeze milk or juice boxes. They do double duty by both keeping your food cold and quenching your midday thirst.

milk

Cheese and yogurt come in individual packages that are oh-so-easy to toss into the box.

Here are some menu ideas for lunch mains, sides, and desserts, with combinations for the five hungry days of your school week. For foods you see listed in orange, find an easy recipe to make (see pages 100–101) or look for a healthy version in the grocery store.

LUNCH MENUS

★ MAINS ★

Egg salad in a pita pocket

Turkey, fresh spinach, and cream cheese in a wrap

Quesadilla (see page 73)

Peanut butter & apple slices on whole wheat

Vegetarian spring rolls

Pasta salad with tuna

Sides

Granola

Minestrone soup

Hard-boiled egg (see page 75)

Sliced carrots & sliced celery

Strawberries & blueberries

Cheese cubes & grapes

Hummus & pita triangles

DESSERTS

Carrot or zucchini muffin

Apple slices dusted with cinnamon sugar

Oatmeal chocolate-chip cookie

Brownie

Chocolate-dipped clementine sections (see pages 88–89)

Weekly Specials

A Week of Lunches

Monday: peanut butter & apple slices on whole wheat, soup, brownie

Tuesday: quesadilla, strawberries & blueberries, carrot muffin

Wednesday: pasta salad with tuna, carrots & celery, oatmeal chocolate-chip cookie

Thursday: vegetarian spring rolls, hard-boiled egg, chocolate-dipped clementines

Friday: egg salad in pita, cheese cubes & grapes, cinnamon apple slices

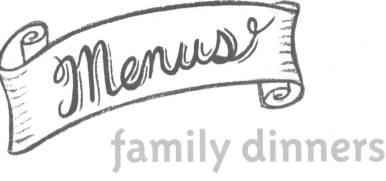

Menus

family dinners

With your cooking know-how, you can easily take charge of dinner. Decide how much time you'll have for cooking, and then make up a menu that fits. Some meals can be made in less than half an hour. Others need a whole afternoon—with friends!

Here are ideas for quick school-night meals as well as relaxed weekend dinners. Try these, or think up combos of mains and sides that you already know your family loves. For foods listed in orange, find a simple recipe to make or look for a healthy version in the grocery store.

School Nights

Easy Cheesy Pasta
- Pasta carbonara—This quick and easy dish mixes pasta with a light, savory sauce of crumbled bacon and Parmesan cheese.
- Green salad with vinaigrette dressing (see pages 84–85)
- Oatmeal cookies (Tip: Make these ahead of time.)

Delish Fish
- Baked salmon with lemon & herb sauce (see pages 82–83)
- Couscous—This rice-like pasta is a snap to fix. No recipe required. Just follow the directions on the package.
- Broccoli stir-fry (see page 86)
- Ice cream

Weekends

A Bit of Little Italy

- Lasagna—This Italian favorite takes a little time to bake, but it's easy and fun!
- Green salad with vinaigrette dressing (see pages 84–85)
- Sourdough bread, sliced
- Berries with whipped cream (Tip: After a rich meal, offer a light dessert, such as fruit.)

Classic Chicken

- Roast chicken (see pages 80–81)
- Seasoned rice (see page 78)
- Green beans (see page 87)
- Fruit cobbler (Tip: Make this dessert earlier in the day.)

Menus

birthday bashes

The best party food is both easy to handle and a fun reflection of your party theme. Build your theme into your menu, like the ideas here, and don't forget the sweet ending! A cake or cupcakes make a birthday official. For foods listed in **purple**, find a simple recipe to make or look for a healthy version in the grocery store.

Picnic Party

Take it outside for a fair-weather feast. Spread out a picnic blanket and set up casual food in baskets, bowls, and platters.

- **Fried chicken drumsticks and thighs**
- Deviled eggs (see page 75)
- **Hummus** with pita bread, cut into small triangles
- Celery, carrots & cucumbers, cut into sticks
- Watermelon, cut into wedges
- **Decorated cupcakes** (See pages 108–109 for icing and decorating help.)

Ice Palace Party

Chill out on the hottest days of summer—or the coldest days of winter. Keep the food and the colors cool in whites, pastels, silver, and gold.

- Tea sandwiches—Small amounts of cucumber and soft butter, smoked salmon and cream cheese, **egg salad,** and other fillings can be pressed between two thin slices of bread and cut into snowflake shapes with a cookie cutter.
- Seedless green grapes
- Ice cream bar—Each guest can create her own ice cream fantasy. Along a counter, set up different flavors of ice cream, sprinkles, chocolate sauce, granola, whipped cream, and sliced bananas.
- **Vanilla frosted birthday cake**—Add pastel sprinkles or shredded coconut. (See pages 108–109 for icing and decorating help.)

Fiesta Time

Colors are bright and the food is spicy in a Mexican-themed party.

- Taco bar—Set out soft tortillas or hard taco shells, cooked ground meat spiced with taco seasoning, shredded cheese, shredded lettuce, sour cream, and chopped tomatoes. Each guest makes her own!
- Quesadillas, cut into wedges (see page 73)
- **Guacamole**
- Corn chips
- Salsa
- Mango wedges
- **Chocolate birthday cake**—Add a dash of cinnamon to the batter before baking. (See pages 108–109 for icing and decorating help.)

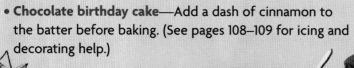

take the cake

A basic iced cake is basically yummy! An iced cake can also be a blank canvas for you to decorate in any way you like—for a birthday or any happy occasion.

Sprinklemania!

Colored sprinkles and decorating sugars give your cake instant pizzazz. Mix them into the icing before you frost the cake, or sprinkle them on top. Or pull out a favorite cookie cutter, rest it lightly on the cake, drop sprinkles into it, and lift it away for a colorful party-themed shape!

Stencils

Have fun with stencils, either homemade or from a craft store. Try hearts, moons, or stars. Hold the stencils just above the frosted cake and dust them with sprinkles, cocoa powder, cinnamon, or confectioners' sugar.

Toppings

Almost anything goes when it comes to cake toppings, as long as they're sweet and can be eaten. **Fresh fruit,** such as sliced strawberries, is always colorful and delicious. Make sure you serve the cake within two hours, though, because the fruit will start to soften. **Shredded chocolate** is also a treat. Use a vegetable peeler to scrape shavings from a good piece of chocolate onto a chilled plate. Then scatter them over the cake.

Other Topping Suggestions:

- Shredded coconut
- Crushed cookies
- Jellybeans
- Hard-shelled chocolate candies
- Gumdrops
- Chopped nuts

Basic Icing

Frosts 24 cupcakes, a 9 x 13 cake, or an 8-inch round layer cake

Ingredients:

Butter 1 cup, softened

Vanilla extract
1 teaspoon

Milk 1 tablespoon
(plus more as needed)

Powdered sugar
32-ounce box or bag

Food coloring
(optional)

Directions:

1. Let the butter sit out at room temperature for at least an hour until it's soft.

2. Use an electric mixer on a low setting to beat together the butter, vanilla, and milk.

3. Gradually add the powdered sugar, and mix until it's smooth. Add more milk if needed, ½ teaspoon at a time.

4. If you want colored icing, add a drop of food coloring and mix. Add one drop at a time until the icing is the color you want.

How to Frost a Cake

1. Make sure the cake is completely cooled before you start.

2. Choose a plate or tray that's at least an inch larger than the cake.

3. Place the bottom layer rounded side down and flat side up on the plate.

4. Lay strips of wax paper around the cake, gently tucking them a bit under the cake.

5. Spread icing on the flat top of the cake layer with a table knife or icing spreader. Don't worry if there are crumbs—no one will see them. But keep them out of the icing bowl.

6. Place the second layer on top of the frosted first layer, *rounded side up.*

7. Place frosting in the middle of the top and spread it out to the cake's edge. Then frost the sides. The wax paper will keep the plate clean.

8. Remove the wax paper strips by pulling them straight out, not up.

9. Decorate!

109

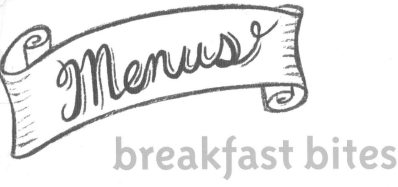

breakfast bites

Nothing says "good morning!" better than a home-cooked breakfast. On a weekend, you have the time to make something special, like pancakes, French toast with fruit, or a frittata—which is a cheesy egg pie with any veggie and meat ingredients you like. (Look for recipes in your favorite places—see pages 100–101.) But what if it's a school day? Here are some quick and easy options to jump-start your morning.

Yogurt & Granola Parfait

This looks fancy, but it's a snap! In a tall cup or glass, add a spoonful of plain yogurt, a spoonful of granola, and a spoonful of your favorite chopped fruit. Repeat until the glass is filled to the top with colorful layers.

Eggs on the Go

Scramble one egg (see page 74) with 2 tablespoons of shredded cheddar or crumbled feta. Scoop it into a pita pocket, add a few leaves of fresh spinach, and away you go!

A Better Bagel

Spread half of your favorite bagel with peanut or almond butter, top with sliced bananas, and put the lid on!

Smoothie

These blender shakes are super-quick, healthy, and oh so scrumptious (see pages 76–77).

Ready-to-Go Oats

Cook steel-cut oatmeal the night before (see the package for easy directions), and stash it in the fridge. In the morning, just pull it out, heat it in the microwave for 1 minute (ask an adult to help), and you have an instant hot breakfast. Top it with cinnamon, raisins, chopped apples or nuts—whatever suits your morning mood.

Oats Notes

Oats come from groats—the grain of the oat plant. Sliced into pieces, groats become **steel-cut oats**. These tasty, chewy oats need to be boiled for about 30 minutes before they're ready to eat. **Rolled oats** have been steamed and pressed—kind of like laundry—so they cook in liquid in just 5 to 10 minutes. You can also soak rolled oats in water or milk without heat. **Instant oats** are pressed into even thinner flakes. With liquid, they cook in just 1 minute.

making a list, checking it twice

You've decided on your menu. You've read the recipes. Now what? It's time to go shopping! But don't dash out the door just yet. You'll save yourself an extra trip or two—and maybe a kitchen disaster (see pages 92–93!)—if you make a list of what you need first.

Step 1: Look at the ingredients lists in your recipes. Put them on your shopping list, including the amount you need. You don't want to get a 10-pound bag of potatoes if a recipe calls for only one small spud. And if you're cooking for more or fewer people than the recipe says, you'll want to keep that in mind when you figure amounts, too.

Step 2: Now look at your menus. Are there any items that don't need a recipe, such as orange juice or a French baguette? Add those things to your shopping list.

Step 3: Take your shopping list into the kitchen. Scout through your cupboards and fridge for each of the items. If you find an item and you have enough of it, cross it off your list. You don't need to buy more.

Step 4: Grab your shopping bags!

Smart Lists

When you make your shopping list, try grouping similar things together. For example, list meats in one place, fruits and vegetables in another, frozen stuff in another. There can be a miscellaneous group, too, for things you don't know how to categorize. When you're in the store, you'll find shopping faster and easier because your list and the store are organized the same way. Fresh fruits and vegetables are all together in the *produce* section. Yogurts and cheeses hang out with other milk items in the dairy cases. Breads and meats each have their places, too.

GROCERY LIST

milk
plain yogurt (1 cup)
shredded cheddar (16 oz)
chicken drumsticks
olive oil
French bread loaf
flour
popcorn
tomatoes can (28 oz)
dog food

apples (3)
mango (1)
romaine lettuce (head)
cherry tomatoes (pint)
garlic (1 bulb)
frozen peas (½ cup)
frozen berry mix (biggest bag)

let's go shopping!

A good cook is a savvy shopper. Get to know all the sections of the grocery store—and how to find the foods in each section that are best for you.

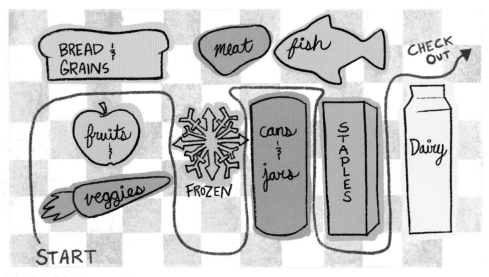

The trick is to understand what's inside the pretty package. And good news: The package tells you. Whether it's a box of mac and cheese, a carton of strawberry yogurt, or a can of chili, everything you need to know is spelled out on the label where it says "Ingredients."

The list of ingredients is required by the government, so look for it. Every ingredient in the package—even water—must be listed, so you really and truly know what you're eating.

Ingredients are listed from most to least. In this can of beans, for example, there are more beans than water, more water than onion, and more onion than salt.

You always want the first ingredients to be a real food, like beans or tuna or peas. What else are you looking for? Answer: a list that is short. Real food doesn't have lots of added stuff. You especially don't want to see chemical names, lots of sugar, artificial flavors and colors, or other ingredients you wouldn't have in your own kitchen.

Your regular grocery store has plenty of fresh, healthy foods. You don't have to go to special stores to find them. Even many foods in the frozen and canned aisles are healthy—and can save time in the kitchen. You know what to do: Just check the ingredients to find the best ones.

Packaged Foods

Many happy and healthy foods come in cans, bottles, jars, and boxes. Beans and tomatoes, oils, vinegar, and other staples are among the fine choices you'll find on the shelves. Healthy grains and pastas, containing just one or two ingredients and nothing else, come in bags and boxes. You can even find foods like soups and sauces that have good-for-you ingredients and no junk.

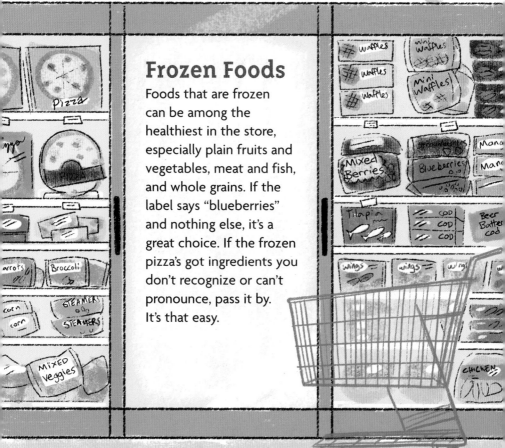

Frozen Foods

Foods that are frozen can be among the healthiest in the store, especially plain fruits and vegetables, meat and fish, and whole grains. If the label says "blueberries" and nothing else, it's a great choice. If the frozen pizza's got ingredients you don't recognize or can't pronounce, pass it by. It's that easy.

Dairy

Milk should say "milk" and maybe vitamins A and D. Other dairy foods include ingredients that turn milk into cheese, yogurt, and more. Compare labels. Better-for-you foods have fewer ingredients—and their names sound like real food, not chemicals.

Sell By?

Most foods have a "Sell By" or "Best By" date on the package. This date tells you the last day the store can sell the food. The food should be good for several more days at home.

SELL BY: 2/11 | 1.5 lbs | PRICE: $6.45

You won't find a list of ingredients on an apple or green bean. But look for a sell-by date on packaged produce, such as salad greens.

MEATS and Seafood

Labels on packaged meat let you know if anything such as water or seasoning has been added. Otherwise, just check the sell-by date to make sure it's fresh.

Going Green

Organic and **sustainable farms** try to keep food as natural as possible and avoid polluting the ground, air, or water. Foods labeled "organic" must follow specific rules made by the government.

Local farms may or may not be organic, but when food travels a shorter distance, it takes less fuel, and that's better for the environment, too.

USDA CERTIFIED 100% ORGANIC PRODUCT

table time

When it's time to take off your apron and enjoy the fruits (and veggies and meats and grains and dairy) of your labors, you want your table to show your creations at their very best.

Places, Please!

To remember the order of a basic place setting, think of the word FORKS. From left to right, it's F for Fork, O and R for the Round plate, K for Knife, and S for Spoon. (P.S. The drinking glass goes above the knife.)

Napkins

Bright napkins liven up a table. If you have many different sets in the drawer, try mixing colors and patterns. Fold or roll them, and place them where you like—to the left, the right, above, or even on the plate itself.

Decorations

Add color with a bouquet of flowers in a vase or pitcher, or small blooms in a row of juice glasses. A bowl of summer fruit, autumn gourds, or evergreens and pinecones makes a pretty seasonal showing. Even toys such as dolls or a train set add a happy touch!

recipe for a chef

Makes 1 happy & healthy girl

Ingredients:

Love of food

Creativity

Enjoyment of hands-on activity

Desire to explore and learn

Attention to detail

Safety awareness

Directions:

1. Take one girl who loves to cook, create, and share what she makes.

2. Add a wide world of recipes.

3. Combine with a delicious assortment of foods, from apples to zucchini.

4. Mix with family and friends.

5. Repeat and repeat and repeat . . .

stories to share?

Tell us about your cooking adventures and discoveries!

Write to:

SGG Cooking Editor

American Girl

8400 Fairway Place

Middleton, WI 53562

(All comments and suggestions received by American Girl may
be used without compensation or acknowledgment.
We're sorry, but we're unable to return photos.)

want recipes?

Make all the foods you love!

This companion for *A Smart Girl's Guide: Cooking* has dozens of recipes for meals, snacks, and parties that are easy to follow and completely delicious. You've got the know-how now. You're the chef!

Use this chart to convert the U.S. measurements in this book to their metric equivalents.

MEASUREMENTS

U.S.	Metric
¼ teaspoon	1.25 ml
½ teaspoon	2.5 ml
1 teaspoon	5 ml
1 tablespoon	15 ml
¼ cup	60 ml
½ cup	120 ml
1 cup	240 ml
1 quart	.95 l
1 gallon	3.8 l
1 inch	2.54 cm
1 ounce	28 g
1 pound	454 g

ml = milliliter
l = liter
cm = centimeter
g = gram

PAN SIZES

Inches	Centimeters
9 × 13	22 × 33
8 × 8	20 × 20

OVEN TEMPERATURES

Fahrenheit	Celsius	Gas Mark
275°	140°	1 (low)
300°	150°	2
325°	165°	3
350°	180°	4 (medium)
375°	190°	5
400°	200°	6
425°	220°	7 (hot)
450°	230°	9
475°	240°	10 (very hot)

Here are some other American Girl books you might like:

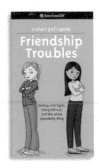

Each sold separately. Find more books online at americangirl.com.

Discover online games, quizzes, activities, and more at americangirl.com